BLACK QUEEN

WITHOUT A THRONE

The Garden in Eden
To America!

John D. Brinson

Resource *Publications*
An imprint of *Wipf and Stock Publishers*
199 West 8th Avenue • Eugene OR 97401

Resource Publications
An imprint of Wipf & Stock Publishers
199 West 8th, Suite 3
Eugene, OR 97401

Black Queen Without a Throne
By Brinson, John D.
Copyright©2003 by Brinson, John D.
ISBN: 1-59244-102-5

Publication Date: 11/27/2002
Revised: 12/5/2003.

Dedicated to my wife Lois, my daughters, Yorlanda, and Seyyida, and to all the dethroned beautiful Black Queens of Africa and the Diaspora.

Contents

Introduction   vii

Part I
Expulsion From The Garden
To Captivity And Degradation   1

Part II
Restoration From Captivity
And Return To The Garden   81

Bibliography   127

Introduction

The only way we can harmonize the story of creation as recorded in the OT of the Christian Bible, with the assertions based on scientific facts that indicate human life began in Africa, is to accept the corresponding implication that Adam and Eve were black, or at least African. This being the case, we can claim the first queen of the earth was a black woman, and Eve was her name according to the Book of Genesis.

Eve and her black king, Adam lived in a "Garden" (territory) provided by God with everything for their happiness and security. But because of the bad decision to disobey the Spirit of God within, in whose image they were created, and submission to the one in the world, they had to reap its accompanying consequences. They lost the joy and security emanating from the presence of God. They lost the Garden of Eden. Their life of happiness and security was replaced with one of spiritual and finally physical oppression in the wilderness of the United States and other places.

Eve and her black king have been completely divested of any knowledge of who they are, and are kept in a state of conflict with each other by racist dynamics. This conflict prevents a basic unity, which would eventually lead to reclamation of "The Garden," and its fruits of joy and security.

Our (black men's) great task is to help bring about an end to the devastating conflict that prevents our spiritual unity with our personal selves and the black woman. Since this conflict derives from a system of total oppression, and we have utilized every peaceful means unsuccessfully so far to bring about the necessary changes, it is now crystal clear that its resolution can only be accomplished through total revolt against the totality of the system that creates and maintains that conflict.

John D Brinson

PART 1
Expulsion From The Garden To Captivity And Degradation

Chapter 1

Fall of the Black Queen

Eve

According to the story of the 'Garden of Eden,' God gave Adam the ruling scepter of the world. He was put in charge and made its ruler and steward. The woman named Eve was provided him as his co-ruler, or queen. This story indicates that God created the first community of humans, man and woman, and provided a territory ("garden eastward in Eden"[1]) rich in the necessary resources for them to survive, prosper, and be happy.

> 28 God blessed them and said to them, "Be fruitful and increase in number; fill the earth and subdue it. Rule over the fish of the sea and the birds of the air and over every living creature that moves on the ground."
> 29 Then God said, "1 give you every seed-bearing plant on the face of the whole earth and every tree that has fruit with seed in it. They will be yours for food. 30 And to all the beasts of the earth and all the birds of the air and all the creatures that move on the ground-everything that has the breath of life

---
[1] Gen. 2:8

in it - I give every green plant for food." And it was so.²

Now, Adam and Eve were living in an idealistic state of innocence, for the Bible informs us they both were naked before each other, un-self-conscious and unashamed. Nudity is used here as a symbol for mutually open and honest self-giving which seems impossible between many black males and females today. However, they lost the ideal state when they allowed the evil entity (Satan, as a serpent) to come between them. Adam lost his ruler-ship, and stewardship of the world and the scepter was passed to the evil one.

If Adam had obeyed God's directive, and not listened to Eve, they would still be the king and queen of the world. But, you see, the evil one* "beguiled Eve," as she listened to him, and from her self-interest, she yielded to the temptation to, "be as God."³ This disobedience and rejection of the God (spirit, residing within⁴) in whom they were imaged, and the submission to the outside, evil one brought about their fall from God's grace. Thence forward they were to suffer the consequences of the choice they made which included their eviction from the "Garden," cursing of the ground, the requiring of exhaustive labor to gain a livelihood, and the imposition of physical death; and in the spiritual realm, the loss of the divine image within, and finally spiritual death.⁵

Lets take a quick observation of those consequences that were reaped by the original pair. First, there was the loss of

---

² Gen. 1:28-31. NIV.
* Personification of negativism, separation from God, and final destruction.
³ Gen. 3:5
⁴ 1 Cor. 3:16. "Don't you know that you yourselves are God's temple and that God's Spirit lives in you?"
⁵ Gen. 3:16-24

territory from which all the resources needed for their survival and improvement were available. It appears that strenuous work to acquire these resources was unknown until after their fall, because God required exhaustive work as a consequence of them making the decision to disobey. Secondly, death was imposed upon them, and it appears that we evidently could live forever in the Garden; thirdly, the loss of the divine image within, and inheritance of the evil spirit image. In other words, instead of acting and doing what God within would have them to do, they began a journey of becoming what the evil image implied. This was the beginning of the fall of the black queen from her God-given position of co-ruler of the world. During her fall, she has tried again, and again to regain this position as can be noted in her intermittent re-elevations as goddesses, and queens in the subsequent ancient civilizations. However, her fall continued until she landed in Hell. Yes, that's exactly where she landed, because if there has been any place at anytime where she has experienced the fires of Hell, it has been in the crucible of slavery as practiced in the United States of America.

Eve's decision, and her successful, persuasion, and control of Adam ushered in their fall. The world's ruling scepter was passed from Adam to the "Evil One", and Adam and Eve were taken out of the "Garden," and prevented from returning by Cherubim guards. This queen appears from the scientific evidence gathered so far, to have been a black woman, and if not black, certainly a dark skin African woman. We are lead to believe by our various scientists, that life began in Africa, and then through various migrations filled the earth.

> Eight to 10 million years ago, most likely in the tropics of Africa, certain venturesome apes gave rise to what were to become erect, bipedal

> creatures: the Australopithec ines. By about two million years ago, one species, a gracile form of Australopithecine appears to have evolved into early human type.⁶

Of paramount interest is the admission of the editors of *Early Man*, that the first man was formed in Africa. Their theory on evolution is of no direct concern to our subject.

Cheik Diop confirms the more than sufficient, scientific evidence that has been published up to the present time to illustrate the fact that Africans were the first people to inhabit and consequently populate the entire planet earth through various exodes. This means that all others who branched off from the so-called, Caucasoid and Mongoloid branches of these original people also have their seminal roots in mother Africa.

> ... we must recognize in all objectivity that the first *Homo sapiens* was a "Negroid" and that the other races, white and yellow, appeared later, following differentiations whose physical causes still escape science. Refusing to accept these facts, scholars substitute hypotheses for them.⁷

Michael S. Williams, in his thought provoking, thoroughly researched, and documented book, *Genesis Revisited*, agrees with Diop, and also locates the Garden of Eden in east Africa, which definitely indicates an occupation by Africans.

> We looked at the research findings of Diop, who in turn based his conclusions on the strength of

---

⁶ *Life Nature Library. Early Man.* New York: 1973, p.57.
⁷ Cheik Anta Diop. *The African Origin Of Civilization*. Connecticut:1917,p.262

Gloger's Law and Leakey's research indicates humanity had its beginnings in that area. Genesis 2:10-13, suggests that the Garden of Eden was located in Eastern Africa.[8]

Most scholars accept Africa as the birthplace of mankind. Many however, influenced by racism, just can't come to believe that black men, those men they hold in utter contempt, built the wondrous, civilization and mysterious pyramids of Egypt. Consequently, they develop highly assumptive, unbelievable, factually, unsupported hypotheses such as visitors from outer space came to earth in earlier times, and directed the building of these civilizations.[*] It's enough to "make you want to holler," at times. They can speculate all they want, but half-baked assumptions and assertions grounded in racism may cause temporary delays, and problems, but can never overcome truth permanently. Truth suppressed will always rise prominently when the moment and proper dynamics demand it.

---

[8] Michael Williams. *Genesis Revisited*. P.26
[*] Robert Charroux. *One Hundred Thousand Years of Man's Unknown History*. N.Y.:1963

Chapter 2

Her Journey
From The Garden

Isis

There was another prominent black queen, the sister and wife of Osiris, the god of ancient Egypt from the earliest of times. She occupied the throne of the world's first, and grandest of civilizations. However, the evil one, Set,[9] devised a plan to kill Osiris, usurp power, and take Isis as his wife.

> Isis was harassed by Set, who was both her half-brother and brother-in-law, a god in the Egyptian pantheon whom the Greeks made equivalent to their Typhon. He plotted, with the twenty-two heads of the Delta nomes (provincial leaders) and with Aso, queen of Ethiopia, to kill Osiris. Set's aim was to seize control of the kingdom and to take Isis for his wife, he being violently in love with her. (Set symbolized the desert to the Egyptians; Osiris the fertile Nile Valley. Set was usually portrayed as red and Osiris as black, when these geographical contrasts were meant.)[10]

---

[9] The "Evil One," in Egyptian beliefs.
[10] St Clair Drake. *Black Folk Here And There*. Los Angeles:1987, Pp.169,170

Osiris was murdered, and cut into many pieces by the evil one. He came down through the annals of history to be associated with death and resurrection, and logically became the subject of philosophical, and theological discussions between the scribes and priests.[11]

> Isis eventually became transformed in the popular mind from the co- discoverer of agriculture in remote antiquity to the symbol of devotion and love of a wife for her husband, a healer, and a nurturing mother. Concurrently, Osiris became the symbol of life after death, of the possibility of a just reward for having lived a virtuous life. Osiris and Isis, with these meanings, became objects of veneration throughout the Hellenistic world.[12]

Isis and her mysteries have been passed down through the ages for the benefit of all mankind today. There are depictions of her that show her as black, and as a prototype of the Christian, Madonna with her Holy Child. Black women in Egypt were held in very high esteem.

> Eleventh Dynasty women evidently played an important part, as is perhaps to be expected in a family living so close to Ethiopian territory, where the queens were more important than the kings. The Pharaohs of this family are represented sometimes with their mothers, or mention them . . ... I cannot help feeling that with the rise of these

---

[11] ibid. 170
[12] ibid, P.170

> southern rulers there comes a strong renewal of the matriarchal practice and importance of women.

After numerous conquests by nomads from the north and their influence, the people began to become lighter in skin color and absorbed many of the conqueror's values and principles. The status of the black woman began to reflect the status of the nomadic women from the north. She began to be viewed and treated in a subservient fashion according to the dynamics of the conquering oppressors' cultural milieu's orchestration and dictation.

Medusa

This is the famous black goddess, whose character and religious importance are maligned, and assassinated in Greek mythology when her supposed snake coiffured head, which has the power to turn anyone who gazes on her to stone, is severed by the mythological, Greek hero, Perseus.[13]

> The terrifying story of Queen Medusa now belongs to the world. The African Medusa, whose name the older generation of lexicographers defined as "Queen," today represents a feminine ideal of beauty. Lexicographers today ignore the meaning of her name. She was the High-priestess of Africa, perhaps also of Italy and Spain.[14]

Her head covered with snakes as depicted when an image is made of her is merely a projected concoction of the Greek

---

[13] "The "Evil One" in that it was his mission to behead her, or better to dethrone her.
[14] Norma Lorre Goodrich. *Priestesses*. New York:1989, p.172

mind. The snakes referred to, was really a crown she wore constructed of "rows of raised cobras' heads," one placed "over the third eye, with the glaring *uraeus*." This attire attests to her powerful, religious and philosophical importance. One can note the image of the cobra on the crowns of many of the pharaohs.

Nefertiti/Nefertari

This venerated, and renown black queen was the wife of the Pharaoh, Akhenaten. This Pharaoh has the distinction of being credited with introducing monotheism to the world. She, Cleopatra, and Isis are the better known of the ancient world's great queens of Egypt. She was co-founder of the famed, and glorious, 18th Dynasty of Egypt. Nefertiti, or Nefertari was elevated to, and worshipped as a deity.[15] Many white scholars and scientists have portrayed this black queen as Caucasian, however she was an African woman. It cannot be over-emphasized that Africa of antiquity was a black continent, populated by black people, and has become modified in skin color only since her occupation by the Hyksos, Greeks, Persians, Romans, Arabs, and other Euro-based white peoples.

Belkis/Queen of Sheba

Queen Belkis, an Ethiopian, or Queen of Sheba as she is known in the Judeo/Christian context, during a visit with Solomon blew his mind with her beauty, impressing him to roll out the red carpet, and spare no expenses for this beautiful, and desirable, Ethiopian Queen.

> The level of hospitality accorded to the Queen of Sheba by Solomon was a tribute to her position

---

[15] St. Clair Drake. *Black Folk Here And There*. Los Angeles: 1987, p.260

and influence. Solomon prepared an apartment built of crystal from the floor to the ceiling for her to reside in. Also he had a throne set up along side his which was covered with silk, fringes of gold and silver, and studded with diamonds and pearls. Gorgeous feasts in halls perfumed with myrrh, gabanum, and incense were lavished upon the Queen of Ethiopia. Solomon was terribly smitten by this Queen and a love affair ensued which led to the birth of their son Menelik who became the first king in the Solomonid line of Ethiopian kings. This line lasted, with a 300-year interruption, until the deposition of Haile Selassie in 1974.[16]

The Christian Bible gives her the name, "Queen of Sheba."[17] The Ethiopians called this queen, "Belkis, or Makeda"[18]

These great Black queens of the past ruled from thrones of black power, in territories provided and protected by black men. Black men, with Black women built these first great civilizations.[19]

Maya

Maya, the mother of Buddha, and *Devaki* the mother of Crishna, were revered as *virgins,* and depicted with the baby Saviours in their arms, similar to the way the Virgin Mary of Christianity is currently represented. "Maya was black and so pure that it was impossible for God, or man to think of her with carnal desire." It is reported, no one could gaze upon Devaki,

---

[16] Ivan Van Sertima. *Black Women in Antiquity. Great Queens of Ethiopia.* Larry Williams and Charles Finch.. New Brunswick:1989, Pp.19,20
[17] 1 Kings 10:1, 2; Chron. 9:1
[18] The Kebra Nagast.Chapter 21-35.Translator: E.A. Budge
[19] Gen 10:8-20

because of the light that invested her." "The gods praised her continually since *Vishnu* was contained in her person."

> Crishna and his mother are almost always represented *black,* and the word *Chrishna* means the black."[20]

These ancient goddesses were black women, whose origin was in Africa. It is through various exodes of their descendants from Africa that their mythos was carried to other locations, throughout the world.

Virgin Mother

Godfrey Higgins, a scholar who visited the cathedrals of Europe before the destruction of most of the Black Madonnas during the anti-religious period' of the French Revolution says:

> The most ancient pictures and statues in Italy and other parts of Europe, of what are supposed to be representations of the Virgin *Mary* and the infant Jesus are *black*. The infant god in the arms of his black mother, his eyes and drapery white, is himself perfectly black.[21]

A source of quite a bit about the black virgin, Godfrey Higgins testifies that during the period 1825-1835, there were several locations where images of the black Virgin were still extant.

> There is scarcely an old church in Italy where some remains of the worship of the *black Virgin*, and *black child*, are not met with, and that the

---

[20] T.W. Doane. *Bible Myths*. USA:1948:Pp. 326,327
[21] ibid., p.235

> pictures in great numbers are to be met with where the white eyes, and of the teeth, and the lips a little tinged with red, like the little black figures in the museum of the India company.[22]

This seemingly, scandalous claim made by Higgins was not based on a single incidence, but rather, on many examples which could readily be observed at many locations, according to T.W. Doane.

> ...the cathedral of Moulins; the famous chapel of "the Virgin" at Loretto; the church of the Annunciation, the church of St. Lazaro, and the church of St. Stephens, at *Genoa;* St. Francis, at *Pisa;* the church at *Brixen,* in the Tyrol; the church at *Padua; the* church of St. Theodore, at *Munich* - in the two last of which the white of the eyes and teeth, and the studied redness of the lips, are very observable.[23]

Today, as you read this book, the Polish people revere the black virgin, *Our Lady of Czestochowa*; there is a representation of the black virgin, *Notre Dame of Kazan* that was carried into battle by the Russian troops in 1612. There is a black virgin at Montserrat called, *Our Lady of Montserrat*, that tradition claims St Luke personally carved.

> The Goddesses Venus, Isis, Hecate, Diana, Juno, Metis, Ceres, Cyble are black.[24]

---

[22] Godfrey Higgins. *Anacalypsis*. Vol.1, p.138
[23] T.W. Doane. *Bible Myths*. USA: 1948, p.336.
[24] Godfrey Higgins, A*nacalypsis*. p.138

The Goddesses Bast, Maat, Mut, Hathor, Nut, Neith (oldest of the gods, who was already born when nothing else existed), and Nephtys were all Egyptian Goddesses and consequently, African and Negroid.

Candace
The Black women who wore this reverent and royal title were some of the greatest military commanders of the ancient world.

It is claimed in one of the traditions that because of her military skills, Alexander the Great on his military march over the ancient world, halted at the borders of Ethiopia. He didn't want to face this formidable foe and face the possibility of defeat and bringing his string of victories to an abrupt end. She Was Empress of Ethiopia in 332 BC.

Queen Kahina
This Black Queen fought against the Arab invaders during the 7th century. She was a nationalist who aroused her people and resisted the attack from the north, the Arab invasion of northern Africa. She and her army forced the Arabs back to Tripolitania.* She prevented the southward spread of the Arabs and their Islamic imperialism into western Sudan. Her death brought to a close, one of the most violent attempts to save Africa from imperialist intruders.

Yaa Asantewa
Queen Mother of Ejisu was the embodiment of the quest for Black liberation. It appears the British colonialist had abducted the Asantehene King Prempeh, and the chiefs had a meeting to discuss how they should make war on the white men and force them to return their king. Some of the chief didn't want war, so

---

* Modern day, Tripoli.

they proposed to go and beg the Governor to bring their king back. Asantewa was present and she stood up and spoke out against the outrage.

> "Now I have seen that some of you fear going forward to fight for our king, If it were in the brave days of Oseim Tutu, Okomfo Anokye, and Opolu Ware, chiefs would not sit down to see their king taken away without firing a shot. No white man could have dared to speak to chief of the Ashanti in the way the Governor spoke to you chiefs this morning. Is it true that the bravery of the Ashanti is no more? I cannot believe it. It cannot be! I say this, if you the men of Ashanti will not go forward, then we will. We the woman will. I shall call upon my fellow women. We will fight the white men. We will fight till the last of us falls in the battlefield."

This fiery, patriotic speech shook the men to their emotional foundation, and they took an oath to fight and struggle with the white men until they release the Asantehene. This was the last of the major wars in Africa led by a woman.

Black women have occupied the most powerful thrones known in the history of mankind. Now, they are oppressed to the bottom of the hierarchal heap. But, since they did it before, then evidently, they can do it again. But, they will need a politically free territory that is secured, and productive of defensive and essential raw materials for progress. She and the black man working together can accomplish that task, and history supports me in that assertion. However, unity is needed. The conflict that exists between them and prevents that unity must be deleted.

This conflict arises in part from the black woman's expectations of the black man in a white male dominated society, and his dismal failure in meeting those expectations. What are those expectations? They are the same as for most women in any society. She expects him to be her protector and provider. This role would be conducive to producing an atmosphere of respect, mutual love, caring, and should produce a feeling of complete faith in, and dependence on each other leading to a powerful, spirit filled, black male / black female unity. Once this unity is formed, there is nothing in this world that can prevent them from accomplishing whatever they will. In antiquity when they were united, they created and gave to the world its first great civilizations (Egyptian, Babylonian, and Indus Valley). However, when they allowed others to drive a wedge between them, they began to fall into disarray and powerlessness, and consequently, have been constrained historically to occupy the lowest rung on the hierarchal ladder in human society. Thus, the black woman is currently, a Queen without a political throne.

She is a queen without a throne because she lost her throne in Eden, and after her capture, forced passage to America, and subsequent, oppression on the plantations, which yet continues today, she has lost her real mind. She has been consistently, especially, sexually exploited since her introduction into the Atlantic slave trade. There was no place, or anyone to turn to for protection. African men's skulls had been opened and all concepts of protecting and providing had been systematically repressed, and covered with negative self-esteem destroying concepts. They were encouraged to develop a childlike dependent personality, have complete dependency on the master, and always obey any command or directive given.

Since the African man had been practically obliterated, and a new creature now existed in his place who did not protect the black woman from the master's whip, or the many rapes perpetrated by both the master and the master's sons, she must have reached a point in her mind where she despised, or at least did not perceive that kind of male as a "man." The black man must have been psychologically, dethroned in her mind. This mental dethronement is still evident, and is acted out daily in their interactions. This forms one of the foundation blocks of the conflict existing between them.

The question that should be on the mind of every thinking black man is; what can I do to help the black woman perceive the black man as her king and begin to respect him? The one most likely to be her "king" on all levels, is the one who can provide protection for her in the broadest sense of its meaning. Many feminists and others may perceive the notion of "protector" and "provider" as sexist, but so be it. Worrying about how others view us has historically been one of our weaker traits and contributed to opening our psyche for reception of negative propaganda from racists and white supremacists. As black men and women we must seize the power and define the correct relationship, which should exist between us. This relationship however, should foster a unified thrust towards the enhancement of our liberation from whatever hinders us from becoming what we are created to be.

A careful analysis of the major conflict causing agents in the current black man/black woman relationship will disclose the rift is caused by the inability of the black man to fulfill the needs, and expectations of the black woman and her corresponding, disrespect for his lack of measuring up.

A protector is something or someone that offers and provides a sense of security when needed. Most male primates provide this protection for the young and females in their families or larger groups. If a lion is to be a successful leader of a pride, he must constantly be on the alert and always ready to protect them from all intruders. This lion is leader as long as he is strong enough to keep leadership of his pride (read, family) and able to protect it. But, as soon as a stronger intruder overthrows him, the pride belongs to the victor. He is free to treat it any way he desires.

This observation is analogous to the black man and his family and racial group in America. After the black man was overthrown and his mind filled with fear and controlled by the system of chattel slavery, he ceased to be a protecting agent of black women. Out of fear of the inevitable, painful whipping, torture, or death that awaited him as the price for protecting black women, the male slave often opted for his personal protection, and survival. Defense of the black female by the black male was not tolerated. However, some black men did defend the black woman and paid the supreme price. An ex slave witness and informer provides the following example of what happens when a black man stands defensively for a black woman who is assaulted by the oppressive slave master, or his agent.

> De only trouble between de whites and blacks on our plantation was when de overseer tied my mother and my father untied her and de overseer shot and killed him.[25]

Lewis Clark, the explorer, also provides us with an example as an intruder invades the marriage of a black man and black woman, thus treating the woman as a common whore and clearly illustrating the failure of this fearful black man to protect his black woman. In referring how a prototype of today's policemen ("patrollers") disregarded the black male half of a

---

[25] FWPSN, Oklahoma, p.28. Quoted in, *From Sundown to Sunup. The Making of the Black Community*. Connecticut, 1972, p.61

relationship and had his way with the defenseless black woman, he states,

> [The] greatest scoundrel is always captain of the band of patrols. They are the off-scouring of all things; the refuse, the fag end, the ears and tails of slavery; the scales and fins of fish; the tooth and tongues of serpents. They are the very fool's cap of baboons, the echo of parrots, the wallet and satchel of polecats, the scum of stagnant pool, the exuvial, the worn-out skins of slaveholders. The are, emphatically, the servants of servants, and slaves of the devil; they are the meanest, and lowest and worst of all creation. Like starved wharf rats, they are out nights, creeping into slave cabins to see if they have an old bone there; drive out husbands from their own beds, and then take their places. They get up all sorts of pretences, false as their lying tongues can make them, and then whip the slaves and carry a gory lash to the master, for a piece of bread.[26]

This type experience had a devastating effect on many of those black women whose dignity was smashed and deprived through being forced to submit to the perverted desires of their masters, the master's sons, the patrollers,* or the black males forced on them by her master on the slave breeding farms.

---

[26] Clark, Lewis. *Narratives of the Sufferings of Lewis and Milton Clark.* Boston: 1843.p.114.

* Sometimes these sexual exploitations were known about, and or, encouraged by black, slave males. It was at least overlooked by most slave males, who wanted to survive.

These women were sometimes sexually exploited by black male slaves, especially was this so in the case of some black slave drivers. Slave driving was an important factor, because it promoted discipline and made sure the work was completed. The masters carefully orchestrated a false sense of power and respect around the position of slave driver. A public ceremony was held and officiated by a Christian preacher and a slave master's power was miraculously, bestowed on the slave driver in the slaves' psyche. Quite a few of these weak minded black drivers must have believed for a while that "they had arrived," and really held "real power," unmindful that power bestowed, is really just power on loan, and can be retrieved at anytime according to the will of the one who bestows.*

> Since drivers were expected to maintain a high level of performance and discipline in the work force, they were charged with meting out punishment to slaves who fell short of the expected standards. Some drivers abused their positions and used punishments not merely to enforce discipline, but as a means of bending other slaves to their will. For instance, a slave woman who rejected the sexual advances of a driver might be assigned an impossible task and then whipped for not finishing it. "If one them driver want you," according to Ben Horry, "they give you task you CAN'T DO. You getting this beating not for you task--for you flesh!"[27]

---

* Our ranks are flooded with this type slave, today. Examples are all around us, and clear examples are many of those holding governmental positions of power.

[27] Charles Joyner. *Down by the Riverside*. Chicago;1985, p.66

A black woman who is subjected to, or witness to the preceding, or similar situation usually hated this despicable type of black man. He of all males should have understood, because they both suffered oppression from the same source. Instead of protecting, comforting and inspiring her, he was imitating and conspiring with the hated master who exploited and tortured them both.

The slave woman was in a situation where the control of her sexual life was external, in that the slave master had complete control of all aspects of her physical being, and through the use of fear also gained control over many aspects of her mind.

A black female ex-slave vividly illustrates the lack of control by the black slave woman over her own sexual and reproductive organ. Ex-slave informer, Rose Williams carried the baggage of hatred for her former slave-master and the black-slave "husband" he forced upon her for many years. She had been traded between a couple of Texas slaveholders. Her new master had not separated her family and had not forced them to work too hard, however; she always carried the baggage of hated of him for forcing a "husband" upon her.

> Dere am one thing Massa Hawkins does to me what I can't shunt from my mind. I knows he don't do it for meanness, but I allus holds it 'gainst him. What he done am force me to live with dat nigger, Rufus,'gainst my wants.
>
> After I been at he place 'bout a year, de massa come to me and say, "You gwine live with Rufus in dat cabin over yonder. Go fix it for livin'." I's 'bout sixteen year old and had no larnin', and I's 'jus' igno'mus chile. I's thought dat him mean for me to tend de cabin for Rufus and some other niggers. Well, dat am start de pestigation for me.

I's took charge of de cabin after work am done and fixes supper. Now, I don't like dat Rufus, 'cause he a bully. He am big and 'cause he so, he think everybody do what him say. We'uns has supper, den I goes here and dere talkin', till I's ready for sleep and den I gits in de bunk. After I's in, dat nigger come and crawl in de bunk with me 'fore I knows it. I says, "What you means, you fool nigger!" He say for me to hush de mouth. "Dis my bunk, too," he say.

"You's teched in de head. Git out," I's told him, and I puts de feet 'gainst him and give him a shove and out he go on de floor 'fore he knew what I's doin'. Dat nigger jump up and he mad. He look like de wild bear. He starts for de hunk and I jumps quick for de poker. It am 'bout three feet long and when he comes at me I lets him have it over de head. Did dat nigger stop in he tracks? I's say he did. He looks at me steady for a minute and you's could tell he thinkin' hard. Den he go and set on de bench and say, "Jus" wait. You thinks it am smart, but you's am foolish in de head. Dey's gwine larn you somethin'."

"Hush you big mouth and stay 'way from dis nigger, dat all I wants," I say, and jus' sets and hold dat poker in de hand. He jus' sets, lookin like de bull. Dere we'uns sets and sets for 'bout an hour and den he go out and I bars de door.

De nex' day I goes to de missy and tells her what Rufus wants and missy say dat am de massa's wishes. She say, "Yous am de portly gal and Rufus am de portly man. De massa wants yu uns fer to bring forth portly chillen."

> I's thinkin"bout what de missy say, but say to myse'f, "I's not gwine live with dat Rufus." Dat night when he come in de cabin, I grabs de poker and sits on de bench and says, "Git way from me, nigger, 'fore I busts yous brains out and stomp on dem." He say nothin' and git out.
>
> De nex' day de massa call me and tell me,"Woman, I's pay big money for you and I's done dat for de cause I wants yous to raise me chillens. I's put yous to live with Rufus for dat purpose. Now, if you doesn't want whippin' at de stake, yous do what I wants." I thinks 'bout massa buyin'me offen de block and savin' me from bein sep'rated from my folks and 'bout bein' whipped at de stake. Dere it. What am I's to do? So I 'cides to do as de massa wish and so I yields.[28]

The experience of the preceding black woman's forced submission to the sexual wishes of the master, really took a heavy psychological toll on her. This 'strong" black woman hated the master and the black man. She must have **hated** that white man because of his control of her uterus and consequently, her future descendants. He decided which male she should reproduce her progeny with, and she had no decision in deciding from which particular gene pool she wanted to draw from, and have flowing through the veins of her future generations. She must have **hated** that black man because he made a decision to participate with their common enemy the white slave-master, in her sexual exploitation and the black race's destruction. It has been shown that the first step in the

---

[28] Herbert Gutman. *The Black Family in Slavery and Freedom*. N.Y.:1977, Pp.84-85.

process of destroying a race or nation is the destruction of its family. The creation of destructive conflict between its men and women will insure division that will tear functional unity asunder.

The black woman was trapped in a system ruled by the white man who exercised complete control in her life, and the man by whom she had historically reproduced herself seemed* powerless to help her. Is it any wonder that at times the rage she feels overflows and is focused on the nearest target, the black male?

An ex-slave female informer, Linda Brent, informs us about the difficulty of a slave woman in preserving her dignity in the wake of her master's desires and demands, which attacked that dignity and produced a state of despair in her spirit.

> Alone in the powerful grasp of the demon slavery; the monster proved too strong for me. I felt as if I was forsaken by God and man; as if all my efforts must be frustrated; and I became reckless in my despair.[29]

The roots of the tentacles of sexual debasement of the black woman had its beginning in the slave forts along the West African Coast line. One historian reminds us that the sexual abuse and control of black female sexuality began in Africa in the slave forts or pens.

We learn from scholars that the quarters for the slave women in one fort is below that of the slave trading gentry, and that at dusk, the black women were forced to assemble in formation in the downstairs courtyard for the slavers to choose which woman they would sleep with that night.

---

* I used the term, "seemed," because in actuality he had the power to help.
[29] Linda Brent. *Incidents in the Life of a Slave Girl*. Boston:1868, P.84

This sexual debasement continued aboard those awful cargo vessels that transported them through the terrible middle passage. As a matter of fact one historian provides information from an observer, John Newton, who claims that as the women and girls in some instances, boarded these ships, the white seamen made their choices of whom they would take sexual advantage of.

> 'When the women and girls' (he writes) 'are taken on board a ship, naked, trembling, terrified, perhaps almost exhausted from cold, fatigue and hunger, they are often exposed to the wanton rudeness of white savages...In imagination the prey is divided on the spot, and only reserved till opportunity offers.'[30]

Out of this total oppression, which is buttressed by fear, developed a strong resentment by the enslaved for the enslavers. Both, the black man and woman resented their masters. This resentment was repressed out of fear and has never found proper expression, and consequently, lies bottled up in their being increasing in pressure with time, as it awaits motivation to explode in the creation of, and discovery of freedom.

If we are to discover what prompted most black slave males to appear defenseless in face of the total attack on the female through whom he reproduces himself, we must note the options he had when making his decision. He had the following two options with their corresponding consequences. 1) He could defend the black woman, and most likely jeopardize his

---

[30] James Pope-Hennessy. *A Study of the Atlantic Slave Trade.1441-1807. Sins Of The Fathers.* N.Y:1967, P.100

life or, 2) he could abdicate his "throne" as protector in her life and become a "boy' in her psyche by deciding to mind his own business and protect himself.

We black men must admit that it has been mostly because of *the black woman's* love, strength, wisdom, and determination that the black race has dared to struggle and still survives today. We must also admit we have acted as less than "men" of other races or groups would have acted in the face of their women being attacked on the same or similar level as black women.

We have witnessed how during chattel slavery to current neo-slavery the black man was/is discouraged from protecting the black woman. This was/is a crucial factor if the white power structure was/is to remain in control of black people. If a group is to be controlled, disunity must be fostered in, and maintained between its men and women. History has recorded for our perusal and consideration, some occasions when in the face of possible death, black men have attempted to defend black women under attack. I have already cited an example of this, but shall cite a more extensive one that should be presented in its entirety, and is long and rather insightful.

> ...near Hamburg, South Carolina, five masked whites broke into Chandler Garrot's home and raped his wife. The native white Mobile police were no better than either the Natchez or Richmond Union Army soldiers. "The enormities committed by these policemen," said Union Army General Thomas Kilby Smith in September 1865, "were fearful. Within my knowledge, colored girls seized upon had to take their choice between submitting to outrage on the part of the policemen or incarceration in the guard-house." The abuse of a black woman that summer especially enraged the black "Alabama," the Mobile correspondent

for the New Orleans Tribune. "Hugh McKeever," the Mobile Advertiser reported on July 31, "was complained of by a negro wench for knocking her down." Alabama law did not permit blacks to give testimony against whites, and the Mobile mayor dismissed the woman's complaint. The mayor and the Advertiser infuriated "Alabama." He asked if the wife of the Advertiser's reporter "is a white wench or a colored lady" and charged that Mobile's mayor lived with a black woman. "How do you feel," he asked of the mayor, "when in the stillness of the night... you return to the bosom of Madame L. and press her to the spot you call your heart.... Do you think of those poor [black] women you have out to work upon the public streets, and still have the heart to say you love and respect one of them?" "Alabama" pleaded that Mobile's black men might "strike for liberty or with the federal authorities to protect the ex-slaves, warned death, justice or blood" and repeat "the scenes of San Domingo" without such protection. He concluded, We have sworn before God to protect inviolate our wives and daughters."[31]

That some black male slaves defended or took a defensive position in relation to assault against slave women is an accepted fact. However, it has always been understood by most black men that a position of defense around the black woman

---

[31] Herbert G Gutman. *The Black Family in Slavery and Freedom*.N.Y:1977 Pp.387-388.

when she is threatened or assaulted is not encouraged nor condoned by this racist system.

Then, there are the vast majority of black men who made the decision to survive in face of the fear they had to overcome in order to protect the black woman, and left her to defend for herself. We need to ask what made them opt out and make this decision? We know fear was the underlying force, but what was the weakness that allowed fear to move in, gain control of our minds and thereby the directions of our actions and reactions? We must answer this question correctly to ensure that we are never that weak again.

This weakness that allowed others to overcome and control us, was our lack of the proper defensive resources. The only way fear can come inside and dominate is if our defenses are too weak or, are missing from our resource arsenal. Let me explain. The black man was stripped of the necessities he needed to protect him, or the women during slave captivity. He lacked the control of a piece of ground, whose terrain he knew, and from which he could receive the proper resources needed for his defense. He needed a secured, sovereign territory that could influence his courage to defend the black woman.

The Black woman's basic conflict with the black man arises out of her belief in her queen-hood, and the black man's miserable failure in securing her a throne to sit on, and land to exploit and rule. This lack of a land base has been the black man's weakness during his entire sad journey in the wilderness of the Diaspora. Scientists have shown us that to insure survival of the fittest, nature has endowed mankind with a strong imperative to secure territory so he will have food and shelter, to attract a mate, safety for the female and her young from predators, and to guarantee a place in the future for the survivor's genes.

> Nature, by instilling in the individual a demand for exclusive living space; insures two consequences: First, that a minimum number of individuals in any population will be enabled to breed in relative security and pass on in fair certainty the conformation of their kind. And second, that the surplus will be cast to the wolves to the owls, to the foxes, to the plagues and famines and lonely, unfamiliar places, there to make the most of perilous conditions or to die.[32]

Now, we must admit, this is exactly the condition of the black man in the Diaspora. He is the outcast; the one who receives the crumbs and drippings at the trough, after everyone else has drank and filled their bellies from the spring of life. He is constrained to a state of dependence on others to supply his needs, because he does not own and control a territory. What stands out in bold relief as the object of the struggle between modern men, and the one thing that is at the root of all his wars and conflict, is territory and status.

I recall a childhood game that most black boys around 9 to 12 years of age in Montgomery, Alabama participated in called the "Hucklebuck Ground." This was sort of a rites of passage modality where manhood and hierarchy were based on physical strength, and or, agility. This game was very simple in its rules and methods. Very simply stated, a territory was marked off, and all the participants entered the territory relying on himself only, with the intent of conquering all others and forcing them to sit in submission, and to remain as the only one standing, as "king of the hucklebuck ground." I have seen several guys end up with broken legs or arms.

---

[32] Robert Ardrey. *African Genesis*. N.Y: 1961, p.39

We went through this leg breaking, ankle fracturing, arm wrenching ritual to establish oneself as ruling monarch of a piece of territory, the "Hucklebuck ground." Many of our black mothers cautioned us, about playing such a rough game, but we nevertheless, played it on regular occasions until the need to play it that way evolved into the way adult men play that game.

When you own or control your own territory, predators are cautious about entering your territory and attacking you since they realize through trial and error, the difficulty in attacking a supposed, prey on its own territory and ending up the winner. A field study on territory was done using animals as models for study, by scholar Robert Ardrey, and it showed that the one who has his own territory has the better chance at surviving the attack of the predator or other enemies.

> Among all the generalizations which one may tentatively put forward concerning tendencies in animal conduct, none rests more firmly on universal observation than Carpenter's own conclusion, that faced by territorial invasion the home team almost always wins. Warfare can be, and must be, continuous along territorial boundaries. Hostility for one's neighbour must be unremitting, and when one meets him at the fence line one must give every evidence of intended rape, pillage, and bloodiest invasion. But when the shouting is all over and perhaps a skull cracked here and there, it is the rule that both sides retire where they came from.[33]

---

[33] ibid., p.105.

If you occupy your own territory your odds of surviving are greatly increased in the face of the predators who want your life. You can provide a sense of protection for the females, and perhaps interest ones who have the qualities you desire and design to reproduce yourself through. If you have no territory you will not have any females to reproduce with. Territory will provide her with food, shelter and a safe environment to birth and raise her young. Territory plays a profound role in providing security to the mother, which puts her in a state where she attends to her young and assists in their survival. However, when she loses the security of the territory, she turns from caring for her young and focuses on herself. The following is an example of problems of fathers, mothers and their young when struggling in a territory-less state. Naturalist C.R. Carpenter moved a colony of monkeys from their territory to Santiago Island and the information he left us of his observations of their subsequent behavior is very insightful for our case.

> One would think that a mother's defence of her young would be an instinct so profound that it would carry on despite any departure from normal life. Nothing could be less true. Without the disciplines of territory and society, mothers scrambled for food without regard for their infants. Time after time the mother fought her own child for possession of a scrap. No male, it goes without saying, rose to the defence of mate or offspring. Without territory, there was only terror. and by the end of the voyage ten infants were dead.[34]

---

[34] ibid., p.87)

Thus we can get a better understanding of why many black men have failed to defend black women and the young in the Diaspora. Now, we know the saying "a mother's love for her children can always be counted on," is true as long as she is on a territory where she feels protected and secure. Without a secure territory, fathers become self concerned, and mothers fight their young for the scarce resources that happens to come their way, you may say that without the security and discipline provided by a territory, the rule of the jungle is in force. It is everyone for himself, and God for us all. It provides for easy disruption of the family unit.

The dynamics of being in our (Black people) condition and oppressed by those who own and control the land that holds us in that condition are so powerful, it would be amazing if we hadn't surrendered more often than not, under the burden of powerful negative forces. By negative force is simply meant, dynamics that influence a person to react as a personification ignorance used against self, as opposed to intelligence, which leads to self- preservation.

The relationship between black men and women is in a negative condition that is buttressed by the black man's demonstration of many negative traits that have replaced those that naturally promote self-reliance, and motivation to protect and provide for black women.* It is with this issue that this study primarily concerns itself. Namely: what is an explanation of the negativisms that many black men manifest in their lives in the that stifles the blossoming of a functional, black male / black female unity   I do not make the claim that black women don't love black men, but rather they do not respect them as they do other men; nor, do I make the claim black men don't

---

* I say replaced, because the natural condition of man is to protect and provide for a woman/women in order to ensure passing his DNA down through generations.

love black women. The claim I make is it is extremely difficult for black women to respect this type of black man. Because of this disrespect, and its dynamics, conflict exists in many relationships.

This tension causing conflict between black couples is caused by the black man's seemingly impotent position in a white male controlled world. The often excessive, critical psychological feedback from the black female, continuously reminding him that he doesn't quite measure up to the definition of "man" in this world doesn't help the situation. This female criticism and lack of respect is justified, and we black men must admit it, so that we can begin the first step towards reconciliation with the black woman. However, it might prove wise to observe the past crises that impacted the black male in such a way that it germinated the negative psychological traits in his personality. Then perhaps, we can let our minds refer a prescription to eradicate the problem, and assist in our healing. This is a dangerous disease affecting so many of our people that the enormity of the problem discourages many of our brothers and sisters.

34

Chapter 3

Uncovering The Past

When a physician attempts to help a client discover the cause, or causes of his/her current emotional problems, he sets out on a journey into the clients past in an attempt to discover a cause (usually a trauma) forceful enough to cause the problem. Likewise, if we are to understand the cause of the negative psychological traits of many black men, we must delve into their past. A logical place to begin is with the traumatic experiences. The change in Africans' personality from positive and healthy to negative occurred within traumatic conditions, during, and during the 15th century, and afterwards in the crucible of the Atlantic slave trade.

American slavery was the most devastating oppression the world has ever known. The slave received no protection from society, religious and secular groups refused to confirm his humanity. In many cases the slave became completely ignorant of, and cut off from his past, and he often lost hope for the future. His existence was within a closed system. The slave's existence depended on the mercy and will of his master. His children were sold, his marriage was not recognized, his wife was often raped, or sold, and he was also subject, without redress, to horrific barbarities. Slave-owners, men and women, as a group appear to have proliferated with sadistic, individuals. This system either destroyed, or profoundly impacted on the slave in such a manner that it reduced human beings to less than

God created them to be. They were treated worse than the master's chickens, cows, horses, and especially his dogs.*

Slavery was a closed system that for practicable reasons destroyed the Africans, and brought into being, persons who were viewed as less than human, and consequently, deliberately, dehumanized and prevented from displaying behavior that authenticated their humanity. It was a system that relentlessly, invaded all areas of the slaves' lives and, negatively modified those behavior patterns that propel towards self-actualization and freedom.

> The slaveholders deprived black men of the role of provider; refused to dignify their marriages or legitimize their issue; compelled them to submit to physical abuse in the presence of their women and children; made them choose between remaining silent while their wives and daughters were raped or seduced and risking death; and threatened them with separation from their family at any moment. Many men caved in under the onslaught and became irresponsible husbands and indifferent fathers. The women who had to contend with such men sometimes showed stubborn cheerfulness and sometimes raging bitterness; they raised the children, maintained order at home, and rotated men in and out of bed.[35]

This information by Genovese contains the components of a paradigm that is still functional today. It is a paradigm of the

---

* There needs to be an exhaustive study on the oppressor and his special relationship with his dog.
[35] Eugene D Genovese. *Roll Jordan, Roll*.N.Y:1972, p.490

current state of affairs of many African men and women in the Diaspora.

In defense of slave men and for your edification, let me share with you the general, scientific Mind bending process slaves were subjected to, and the processes' goal. We are advised by, Kenneth M. Stampp, that there was a systematic five-step process whose goal was bringing into being a new creation.

1. Establishing and maintaining strict discipline.
2. Create in them a consciousness of personal inferiority.
3. Awe them with a sense of their master's enormous power.
4. Persuade them to accept and imitate the master's standards.
5. Impress him with his helplessness and create in him a perfect dependence on his master.[36]

In many instances the process was successful, and I am persuaded that some of these black males consciously acquiesced to the white slave master, only because of his superior armament, but remained his opponent as opposed to becoming his new creations. However, many male slaves succumbed totally to the program out of fear and ignorance, and lost their African self, and were re-born negroes. A negro is a caricature of the master's conception of an African within the chattel slave system, and as many Africans 'acted' the role, many however, internalized this concept, and in fact, became the master's new creation, a negro. What is a negro? A negro is exclusively, a European and its descendants' creation utilizing stereotypes and caricatures, and imposing them on the captive and landless Africans to instill inferiority in them. What is so dastardly wrong with this concept is it has been so thoroughly

---

[36] Kenneth M Stamp. *The Peculiar Institution*. N.Y:1956,p.144-147

embedded in many of our minds, that its legacy is still with us, and it appears its complete demise may be way off in the future. Richard B. Moore informs us that,

> ...when a name which has been connected with images and other associations in the human mind arises in the consciousness, it immediately calls forth reactions with which the name is associated.[37]

When this degrading term is propelled from racist lips and assaults the consciousness of its intended victim, immediately the air becomes charged with pain and anger emanating from the depths of the targeted victim's soul. The victim of this humiliating verbal attack can do one of two things: 1. He can internalize the pain and anger, and, or react stereotypically, or, 2. He can explode emotionally and physically finding release from his oppressive emotional condition.

   I have eventually come to understand, that life is really very simple. Its simplicity lies in the fact that it offers only two decisive roads as we travel through our life's mission. One is hope and the other is despair. Depending on which choice we make determines to a large extent the quality of life we experience. We have the responsibility of constantly, every conscious moment of our lives, of making one of these choices and reaping its consequences. During the harsh, torturous reality of chattel slavery many choices made by our male ancestors were for personal survival. A program of reward and punishment utilized by the slave master heavily influenced them. If they complied in a subservient manner, eagerly completing the task the master demanded, they might receive an

---

[37] Richard B. Moore. *The Name "Negro" Its Origin And Evil Use."* Baltimore:1992.

old hat, or a discarded coat that the master had personally worn as a reward. Evidently, however, these wretched souls believed the choice made was the right choice when made, because it allowed them to survive for another day. These choices often included becoming samboes, (pimping, sexual promiscuity, absent fathers, child-like behavior, low achievement, etc.). It was the Africans' experiences beginning from their capture in Africa to slavery on the plantations that acted more forcibly (traumatic) on their psyche than those of the more distant past.

We bring to our current experiences here in the United States, all of our past experiences. We experience the present the way we do because of past experienced dynamic social determinants. Consequently, as Gunnar Myrdal has observed,

> The effect of a new experience is not simply one of addition or subtraction, since an individual defines this experience in terms of all his previous experiences. [38]

How the African American defines his experience is determined primarily by traumatic experience marks alone his journey to the plantations. Let us observe several of those bold marks of the not too distant past. The period of slavery contributed to several marks that can easily be discerned as traumatic enough to act as powerful dynamics of influence on all subsequent experiences of the slaves.

The first traumatic experience was the disruption of the village and the conquering or kidnapping of the person, transforming his mental and physical reality from freedom to captivity. The following example aptly describes the trauma to the emotions of an individual elicited by an immediate, and

---

[38] Gunnar Myrdal. *An American Dilemma* Vol 1, N.Y.: 1944, p.151

forceful separation from her familiar surroundings, or family and marched off in coffles from hundreds of miles in the interior to the west coast. Mungo Park left the following graphic illustration of this fact.

> One of the slaves had been finding it hard to keep going the last three days. As they entered a town, it was evident he could go no further, and his master resolved to trade him for a young slave girl belonging to one of the townspeople.
> Early in the morning, the girl came out with some other young women to see the caravan off She had no idea of her fate until her master took her by the hand and delivered her to her new owner. Her gay expression changed. **Terror** and **distress**[39] took hold of her as a load was put on her head and a rope placed around her neck. It was pitiful to hear her wild farewell to her friends.[40]

The trauma from the immediate separation from familiarity, and the ripping up by the roots of emotional bonds that develop in close relationships pushed the victim to her emotional limits. This was a significant emotional experience that affected all of her future experiences. One of the worst fears, the African in the coffle had besides not knowing where he was going was the fear of not being able to keep up, and consequently left by the rest of the coffle on the road to die. If you multiply this by the millions who had this experience, you can begin to understand its magnitude and importance.

---

[39] Emphasis mine.
[40] Quoted by; Anne Terry White. *Human Cargoes. The Story of the Atlantic Slave Trade*. Champaigne, IL:1972 ,pp.56,57

The second traumatic experience was the middle passage during which the beginning of the destruction of the African's humanity began.

Rev. John Newton, the Captain of one of those ships that transported the captive Africans, informs us of the size of the room down in the ship's hold the captives were packed in.

> The cargo of a vessel of a hundred tons or a little more is calculated to purchase from 220 to 250 slaves. Their lodging rooms below the deck which are three (for the men, the boys and the women) besides a place for the sick, are sometimes more than five feet high and sometimes less; and this height is divided toward the middle for the slaves lie in two rows, one above the other, on each side of the ship, close to each other like books upon a shelf. I have known them so close that the shelf would not easily contain one more.[41]

These captives were fortunate because if the hold had been six feet deep instead of five feet another shelf would have been added above the other and each captive would have had less than twenty inches of headroom.

Our imaginations cannot fathom the depths of despair and the tremendous anxieties such closeness must have elicited from the emotions of these poor souls who had been snatched from their families and forcibly separated from them forever. Can you imagine how many of them drifted into the realm of insanity, or death to escape the pain and brokenness they felt? Captain John Newton adds:

---

[41] John Newton. *Thoughts Upon the African Slave Trade*. London:1788.

> The poor creatures, thus cramped, are likewise in irons for the most part, which makes it difficult for them to turn or move or attempt to rise or to lie down without hurting themselves or each other. Every morning, perhaps, more instances than one are found of the living and the dead fastened together.[42]

These poor wretched souls were packed in such a way that each one's area was so tight they had to lie in some instances, curled against one another like spoons in a drawer, or stacked like sardines in a flat can. The very closeness with filth and diseases aggravated the situation. When it stormed, and the ship rocked and rolled incessantly, sickness permeated the thick, hot air in the holds where they were kept. If a slave on the top platform became nauseated or suffered diarrhea it cascaded or splashed down on the slave occupying the lower platform. Can you imagine the tremendous depression of the spirit and hopelessness these slaves must have experienced?

The third traumatic experience germinated during slavery on the plantations. This period of slavery has been heavily documented with reports of daily torturing of the slave using some techniques only a depraved mind could have invented. A member of the white race, Theodore Weld, a white citizen, left us the following account of the depravity of the slave master's morals and his disrespect for African representatives of humanity.

> We will prove that the slaves in the United States are treated with barbarous inhumanity; that they are over-worked, under-fed, wretchedly clad and..., made to wear gags in their mouths for hours

---

[42] Ibid.

or days, have some of their front teeth torn out or broken off, that they may be easily detected when they run away; that they are frequently flogged with terrible severity, have red pepper rubbed into their lacerated flesh, and hot brine, spirits of turpentine, &c., poured over the gashes to increase the torture; that they are often stripped naked, their backs and limbs cut with knives, bruised and mangled by scores and hundreds of blows with the paddle, and terribly torn by the claws of cats, drawn over them by their tormentors that they are often hunted with blood hounds and shot down like beasts, or torn in pieces by dogs; that they are often suspended by the arms and whipped and beaten till they faint, and when revived by restoratives, beaten again till they faint, and sometimes till they die; that their ears are often cut off, their eyes knocked out, their bones broken, their flesh branded with red hot irons; that they are maimed, mutilated and burned to death over slow fires.[43]

The masters of the plantations did not torture their slaves just for the sake of torturing, but with the objective of instilling fear in them and bringing them under complete control. However, there are reports of some masters being so perturbed by their slaves that they bite them. Fear and pain worked as a deterrent from certain behavior and a motivator to help the slave decide to become what the master projected and taught him to be.

---

[43] Theodore Weld. *American Slavery. American Slavery as it is.* New York: 1839. P
p.9,10.

It was within the literal hell of the Atlantic slave trade, beginning with the African's capture; to their removal from familiar surroundings; to the horrid middle passage; through the plantations, and down to today, that the negative personality types have their origin and maintenance.

Let us observe the role fear played in controlling the slave, and making it possible for the masters to more easily train the slave to totally submit to their superiority, wishes, and commands.

Chapter 4

The Fear Factor

Fear was utilized as the controlling factor to encourage the black man and woman to act and react in a manner that pleased the master, and insured their survival in the terrorist, system of slavery. Fear of the torture of the lash, and ultimately, fear of death the slave-masters and others could unleash on them at the slightest provocation was the tool by which the slave was forced to submit to the slave-master's authority. Kenneth M. Stampp informs us of the master's utilization of fear as a principle in gaining complete control of, and absolute submission of the slave.

> The only principle upon which slavery could be maintained, reported a group of Charlestonians, was the "principle of fear." In his defense of slavery James H. Hammond admitted that this, unfortunately, was true but put the responsibility upon the abolitionists. Antislavery agitation had forced masters to strengthen their authority: "We have to rely more and more on the power of fear. . . . We are determined to continue masters, and to do so we have to draw the reign tighter and tighter day by day to be assured that we hold them in complete check." A North Carolina mistress, after

Subduing a troublesome domestic, realized that it was essential "to make them stand in fear"[44]

Fear was induced in the slave because it made the slave stand in awe of the powers and authority of the master. The master made the laws, and interpreted the laws he had to obey. The master devised rules, by which he governed his slaves in his private empire (plantation) in order to accomplish his goal; their perfect submission, and the producing of profits for him. To accomplish this goal, he dedicated himself to making them "stand in fear" of his absolute power over every nook and cranny of their lives.

The slaves were legally[*] reduced to the status of private property of their owners. They belonged to the owner just as his cattle, home, and other items. You might say and be correct, that the slave owner had free will to do, anything imagined and he desired with his chattel. The master stood more or less, as a god in their lives as he pompously, dispensed rewards or punishment according to his will. In their lives he occupied the seat of power of life or death over them. He supplied them food and clothing, and made and kept them economic dependents of his. He was their most immediate, and constant concern.

One thing the slave system did for sure, during the "breaking in period" and throughout the chattel slave period, was it grinded out the "manliness" of many African males and reduced them to obedient chattel. This was accomplished mostly through the instillation of fear by the regular use of the whip and worse things. However, the whip was the primary tool used to instill fear of the white masters[*] them.

---

[44] Kenneth M. Stampp. *The Peculiar Institution*. New York:1956, P.146
[*] This was accomplished, with the sanctioning of the U.S. government.
[*] White god, or white race.

Frederick Douglass has informed us that their owner could use any pretense or whatever to whip or order the slave whipped.

> For instance, if a slave looked dissatisfied, it was said, he had the devil in him, and it must be whipped out. If he spoke too loudly when spoken to by his master, it was said that he was getting too high-minded. If he forgot to remove his hat at the approach of a white person, he was wanting in reverence, and had to be whipped for it. If he ventured to vindicate his conduct when censored for it, he was guilty of impudence. If he, while plowing, broke a plow, he was considered careless. Masters seldom failed to take advantage of such opportunities.[45]

Frederick Douglass further claims,

> A mere look, word, or motion-a mistake, accident, or want of power-are all matters for which a slave may be whipped at any time.[46]

Douglass also claims the masters even used murder to instill fear and control in their slaves' lives. He impresses on us the understanding that the installation of fear in the slave was the highest of importance in the maintenance of the system and an integral part of it.

An ex-slave informer named Charles Ball reports of a situation in which the master utilizes the torture of the water on a female slave as an object lesson in fear and control over him.

---

[45] Frederick Douglass. *Narratives*. Boston: 1845. pp. 79-80)
[46] Ibid, pp 79-89

The following is his description of the method used and the pain and suffering induced in that woman during the event.

> When the water first strikes the head and arms, it is not at all painful; but in a very short time, it produces the sensation that is felt when heavy blows are inflicted with large rods. This perception becomes more and more painful, until the skull bone and shoulder blades appear to be broken in pieces. Finally, all the faculties become oppressed; breathing becomes more and more difficult; until the eyesight becomes dim, and animation ceases. This punishment is in fact a temporary murder; as all the pains are endured, that can be felt by a person who is deprived of life by being beaten with bludgeons.[47]

One thing we can agree on is that fear was consistently used as an important primary tool for controlling the slave's actions, and consequently his life. The following information was left to us by, Dr C.L.R. James:

> The slaves received the whip with more certainty and regularity than they received their food. It was the incentive to work and the guardian of discipline. But there was no ingenuity that fear or a depraved imagination could devise which was not employed to break their spirit and satisfy the lusts and resentment of their owners and guardians.[48]

---

[47] Charles Ball. *Slavery in the United States*. 1837. p.500
[48] CLR James. *The Black Jacobins*. N.Y: 1962. p.12

Dr James also mentions the mutilations and other tortures the slaves were subjected to so they would be disciplined, and under the complete control of others. He states that sometimes the broken flesh created by the painful lacerating lashes was not enough pain in the master's mind, and he added to the pain by pouring peppers and using other harsh, irritants to make the pain even more excruciating. He states,

> Whippings were interrupted in order to pass a piece of hot wood on the buttocks of the victim; salt, pepper, citron, cinders, aloes, and hot ashes were poured on the bleeding wounds. Mutilations were common, limbs, ears, and sometimes the private parts, to deprive them of the pleasures, which they could indulge in without, expense. Their masters poured burning wax on their arms and hands and shoulders, emptied the boiling cane sugar over their heads, burned them alive, roasted them on slow fires, filled them with gunpowder and blew them up with a match;[49]

Can you imagine the impact you would have experienced had you witnessed a fellow man, a comrade being "burned alive," or "roasted on slow fires," as punishment and an object lesson to you? The slave master ruled with absolute power within the context of the slaves' lives. This absolute power was grounded in and maintained by **fear**. It succeeded in causing many slaves to stand in absolute fear of the White master. It is amongst the many negative, legacies the current, and future generations must deal with, because it is the primary negative factor that acts as a bulwark against our attaining liberation.

---

[49] ibid. p.12.

50

Chapter 5

Breaking The Male's Will Of Resistance

They prepared the will (spirit) of the African by the use of pain, to submit to fear. We have statements from scholars that after many masters whipped them, they would pour "red pepper," and other irritants such as "turpentine"[50] in their lacerated wounds to inflict as much pain as possible. The masters "burned them alive," and "roasted them on slow fires,"[51] and also reports they even "filled them with gunpowder and blew them up with a match."[52] Fear of this kind of horrendous pain experienced by many influenced them to become submissive in order to avoid pain or death. The master held absolute power in the minds and lives of slaves. This understanding and its acceptance caused them to view the slave master as a god.

Concomitantly, the master infected the minds of the Africans by thoroughly, convincing many of them of his superiority and their inferiority. Once the master gained control of their minds, their wills usually obeyed the choices made by it. The mind usually concluded from past experiences that in order to escape seemingly unbearable pain, acquiescing, or not to the master's demands and instructions would be the chief determinant. Usually, when the mind makes a decision; the will

---

[50] Theodore Weld. *Introduction to American Anti Slavery*. American Slavery as It is. P.9
[51] CLR James. *The Black Jacobins*. P.12
[52] Ibid. p.12.

determines whether it will be acted out or not. Fear of the inevitable inhuman, excruciating pain the master would bestow on them, weakened, or breached the wills of many black men.

Now, any so-called, "normal," or "macho man" for that matter, reading this topic must agree that had they been the unfortunate recipient, or witness to those horrible whippings, mutilations and tortures, they would have been grabbed by fear and controlled by it every moment of their remaining conscious existence. Fear is the one emotion that most black male slaves must have constantly experienced. It is this fear factor and its symptoms, which raises its ugly head in the black man/black woman relationship. It has rendered many black men impotent failures when it comes to **protecting** the black woman. This is no modern phenomenon, but has its origin in the fear infested chattel slavery system.

Two very clear examples of this fear phenomenon working itself within the psyche of many black men are, number one, if black men were not filled with fear of the white man, they would be righteously struggling for total liberation from their oppressors, utilizing all methods and placing physical survival on the line for it. Number two, those angry young men who should be our soldiers are on the contrary constantly visiting violence on other black people at the slightest provocation, and very seldom towards white people as representatives of the oppressor. Why do some adult black men mentally and physically abuse black women, and turn into 'grinin,' 'effete,' 'shufflin,' "sambo" acting clowns in the presence of white men and women? It is the fear of the white man based on his ability, and seemingly willingness to cause him a lot of pain or annihilation. The stereotype "Sambo" germinated in the minds of slave masters and was projected into the minds of African slaves.

Chapter 6

Negative Personality Types

Sambo/Rustus/Coon, et al.

This was/is a most powerful stereotype and we have seen this type in all levels of African American men. It has been noted in men from intellectuals to the unlettered ghetto brother in our lifetime. However, it is important to note that the "sambo" type never existed in Africa, nor has come into being in the West Indies, or any place in the Diaspora the captured Africans were forcibly carried to for oppression. The sambo personality is a United States of America phenomenon, exclusively. It was a role created by the master, acted out by the slaves and reinforced by the master's use of punishments or rewards. It was an effort on the part of the "sambo," slave to acquiesce to his totally oppressive situation. It was essentially a role portraying the projected negative, conceptions of the slave masters. It was the case of some black man adjusting to the stress of a possible painful, punishment so he acted and conformed to the various master projected negative stereotypes of, laziness, stealing, lying, promiscuity, dependant, and etc.

It must be remembered, that many Black men were either acting (dramatizing) or refused to play the role. Otherwise, how could we account for revolutionaries, such as the 'slave' in South Carolina, Reverend Nat Turner? Nat Turner was the kind of man who wanted and acted for his freedom in such a way, it caused fear and trembling to ripple throughout the slave-holding southern states.

Stanley Elkins, leaves us with the following information on the slave master's perception of the personality of "sambo."

> The characteristics that have been claimed for the type come principally from Southern lore. Sambo, the typical plantation slave, was docile but irresponsible, loyal but lazy, humble but chronically given to lying and stealing; his behavior was full of infantile silliness and his talk inflated with childish exaggeration. His relationship with his master was one of utter dependence and childlike attachment: it was indeed this childlike quality that was the very key to his being. Although the merest hint of Sambo's "manhood" might fill the Southern breast with scorn, the child, "in his place," could be both exasperating and lovable.[53]

The role of "sambo" was a fixture in the white race's consciousness as was illustrated by its matter of fact usage by the supposedly liberal, and prestigious, New York Times' greetings to our recently emancipated African-American slave ancestors in May 1865.

> "The negro misunderstands the motives which made the most laborious, hard-working people on the face of the earth clamor for his emancipation. You are free, Sambo, but you must work! Be virtuous, too, oh, Dinah! 'Whew! Gor Almighty! Bress my soul!'"[54]

---

[53] Stanley M Elkins. *Slavery*. N.Y. 1959, p.82
[54] Herbert G Gutman. *The Black Family in Slavery and Freedom*. N.Y:1976, p.301

The New York Times Newspaper served an important function by giving life to, and perpetuating the racist stereotype, "*Sambo*." There has been a flood of businesses that used this image as a central focal point in advertising; Hollywood has used this demeaning symbol in many movies;* it has also been used in books, and on stage. It was used as toys and household items. But, worst of all it has been accepted and propagated by many black men as they shuffled into this role for personal advantage. This image was utilized so relentlessly that it appeared to some as the true depiction of the black man's character and personality. Many black men internalized this concept of themselves, and acted out the role to perfection when the situation called for it. The tragedy is, many of these men acted the role so long until it became a automatic reaction when the necessary dynamics were doing motivating.

Pimping

Historian, James Pope-Hennessy reminds us that during the period of chattel slavery, female house slaves were looked upon as convenient sexual tools for the master, his sons, and others of the master's choosing that provided the greatest contributions to the beginnings of the pimp in the African American community.

> Their masters, who made them available to inexperienced adolescent sons and to male houseguests, looked on Negro girls and young women employed about the house as fair game. Negro valets and footmen acted as agile and experienced pimps.[55]

---

* The "Stephan Fetchet" (step and fetch it) character is an example.
[55] James Pope Hennessy. *A Study of the Atlantic Slave Trade*. N.Y: 1967, p.133

I can imagine valets and footmen, considered themselves a different class slave than the field slave. They were close to the master and escaped the hard work in the field. Some of them must have believed that some how they had arrived or were arriving, and consequently, would do anything to please the master. Footmen and valets were house slaves. Malcolm X has advised us of the behavior of some of those house slaves. He said the house slave identified so with the master until, if the master became ill the slave would ask, "what's the matter boss, we sick?" So it should not come as a surprise to you, that some male house slaves would act as pimps between the slave master and some slave women. These black men were doing what they perceived as necessary for personal gain, and survival in an oppressive and treacherous situation.

Sexual Promiscuity

It appears that the practice of sexual promiscuity is rampant in a portion of the black male population of the United States. It is noted as a component in connection with the break up of many black families. We must remember the majority of the captive Africans were indigenous to the west coast of Africa. In connection with this, there wasn't any need for sexual promiscuity because the cultures of the west coast African allowed for a system of marriage called polygamy. Under this system a man could have as many wives as he could afford. There wasn't a real need for the male to be sexually promiscuous, that is, to habitually have sexual relations outside the marriage. Consequently, the trait of promiscuity in the black male has its beginning in the United States during the infamous Atlantic slave trade. A slave informer, Lewis Jones provides the following illumination on the encouragement of promiscuity by the slave-masters.

> My mammy am owned by Massa Fred Tate and so am my pappy and all my brudders and sisters. How many brudders and sisters? 'Lawd A:mighty! I'll tell you, 'cause you asks, and dis nigger gives de facts as 'tis. Let's see; I can't 'lect de number. My pappy have twelve chillun by my mammy and twelve by anudder nigger, name' Mary. You keep de count. Den, dere am Lisa. Him have ten by her. And dere am Mandy. Him have eight by her, And dere am Betty him have six by her. Now, let me'lect some more. I can't bring de names to mind, but dere am two or three others what have jus' one or two chillun by my pappy. Dat am right-close to fifty chillun, cause my mammy done told me. It's disaway: my pappy am de breedin' nigger.[56]

The master promoted sexual promiscuity in the male slave by using many of them as breeders with women they had chosen for them and not recognizing marriages. Quite often, many males had upwards of dozens of women appointed to them by the master for breeding, and sexual enjoyment. Listen to the words of slave informant Elige Davison.

> Massa, he bring some more women to see me. He wouldn't let me have jus' one woman. I have 'bout fifteen and I don't know how many chillen. [Some number] over a hunerd, I'se sho'.[57]

It appears that it was because of the state of the slave family, that black male slaves have the genesis of their sexual

---

[56] James Mellon. *BullWhip Days. The Slaves Remember*..N.Y.:1988, p.149
[57] Donna Wyant Howell. *I Was A Slave*. Wash. DC:1996.p.12.

promiscuity. It appears that the most of the slave's families were matrilineal in form and practice The mother was of more importance than the father in her duties associated with her family. In many cases a slave mother (without a husband) and her children was considered a family.

A central factor that contributed enormously to sexual promiscuity was the intended design of the system of relationships between the slave mother and the father of her children. As happened more often than not, slave parents were often separated by the capricious decision of the master to sell them to different slavers from different locations. This fact alone put a tenuous slant on all black male/female romance relationships. Because of being sold several time and separated from the mothers of his children as many times, it would have been a big surprise if they hadn't developed promiscuous tendencies. Kenneth Stampp claims,

> The general instability of slave families had certain logical consequences. One was the casual attitude of many bondsmen toward marriage; another was the failure of any deep and enduring affection to develop between some husbands and wives.[58]

So, out of being shifted from place to place, and separated from one wife, or partner after another, many males developed and maintained a sense of detachment from the female, because as slaves, tomorrow was not promised for them to still be together. Tomorrow was pregnant with the possibility of being sold and separated from each other forever. Within these dynamics the male's primary role, and responsibility was

---

[58] Kenneth M. Stampp. *The Pecular Institution*. N.Y.:1956, p.345.

fathering children by all of his wives (mates) wherever he ended up after relocation by sale. This was a widespread practice and it promoted the practice of irresponsibility amongst many black men towards their children and the children's mothers.

Absent Father

Most often than not, when a male and female considered themselves married and were the recipients of children, they were often separated from one another because of the sale of one or the other. Sometimes the separation was but a few miles and at others it was as far as a different state. Even when it was just a few miles, the system was designed to discourage the marriage. It was against some of the most difficult obstacles that many fathers overcame to visit their families. Herbert Gutman synthesizes the descriptions of some of these visits as provided by children in South Carolina.

> "My pappy," said one," had to git a Pass to come to see mammy. He slipped in and out 'nough times to have four children." "My pa," explained Millie Barber,",. come sometimes widout de pass. Patrollers catch him way up de chimney hidin' one night; they stripped him right befo' mammy and gave him thirty-nine lashes, wid her cryin' and a hollerin' louder than he." "A man dat has a wife off de place," admitted Caleb Craig, "see little peace or happiness. He could see de wife once a week, on a pass, and jealousy kep him 'stracted de balance of de week, if he love her very much."[59]

Many times the husband was sold and separated from his mate and carried to another State, he more likely took up with

---

[59] Herbert G Gutman. *The Negro Family in Slavery and Freedom*.N.Y: p.137

another mate and started another family. When he is sold again and separated from that family to another master never to see them again, he begins to grow in his new found role of "Rollin' Stone."

Emanuel Ryer, a slave informant sheds light on the practice of masters creating slave families headed by females. This was accomplished during the process of slave breeding. The master would select which male would breed with which woman. Quite often he would have paired the poor woman with as many different men as she had children.

> Well, just like I tell you, slavery chillun had dey daddy somewhe' on de plantation. Cose dey had a daddy, but dey didn' have no daddy stayin' in de house wid demo White folks would make you take dat man whe' if you want him or no. Us chillun never didn' know who us daddy been 'til us mammy point him out' cause all us went in Massa Anthony Ross' name. Yes, ma'm, all us had a different daddy, so my mammy say.[60]

This role required him to move from one relationship to another with women, and making sure not to tarry long enough with any to allow "grass to grow under his feet."

Dependant - Low Achiever

This type was created during slavery and results from being separated from a territory he owned and controlled. It can be noted conspicuously amongst those men who make a life begging, or waiting on the government to provide them what it determines they should receive.

---

[60] Donna Wyant Howell. *I Was A Slave*. Washington DC:1996. p.12

Slavery in most instances destroyed our ancestors' need to achieve. There was no incentive for their self-achievement. They were in a state of total dependency on the masters of the plantations. Vestiges of this dynamic have been continued down to today. Thomas Pettigrew provides his analysis of the reasons for low achievement among many African Americans:

> Negroes in bondage, stripped of their African heritage, were placed in a completely dependent role. All of their rewards came not from independent initiative and enterprise, but from absolute obedience to a situation that severely depresses the need for achievement among all people.[61]

After emancipation many of our ancestors continued the behavior of dependency. There is a direct historical connection between our present state of dependency and our ancestors' dependent conditions during slavery. When modern black men allow someone else, especially if that someone has demonstrated he is the main enemy to both, control and supply his shelter and food, and disperse it to him according to their will, as a recipient he is responding to a trained behavior that started centuries ago, and that behavior has finally evolved into a psychological trait.

The animosity between the slave male and female was created and maintained by the slave master and his children. During the earliest years, a slaver from the West Indies brought his practical knowledge on controlling slaves to the United States. The West Indies is the notorious place where the

---

[61] Thomas Pettigrew, *A Profile of the American Negro* (Princeton, NJ: 1964) p. 14.

"Breaking in" of the newly arrived Africans took place. This "breaking in" was a training process that reduced once fierce African warriors into slaves. This slaver from the West Indies provided the outline for the division of all slaves from one another. So, you see the division between the black man and woman is part of, and the result of the systematic implementation of programs specifically designed to drive a wedge between all black people, and destroy any semblance of unity. The following is his program.

> Gentlemen:
> I greet you here on the bank of the James River in the year of Our Lord one thousand seven hundred and twelve. First, I shall thank you The Gentlemen of the Colony of Virginia for bringing me here. I am here to help you solve some of your problems with slaves. Your invitation reached me on my modest plantation in the West Indies where I have experimented with some of the newest and still oldest methods for control of slaves. Ancient Rome would envy us if my program is implemented. As our boat sailed south on the James River, named for our illustrious King, whose version of the Bible we cherish, I saw enough to know that your problem is not unique. While Rome used cords of wood as crosses for standing human bodies along its old highways in great numbers, you are here using the tree and the rope on occasion.
>
> I caught the whiff of a dead slave hanging from a tree a couple miles back. You are not only losing valuable stock by hanging, you are having uprisings, slaves are running away, your crops are

sometimes left in the field too long for maximum profit, you suffer occasional fires, your animals are killed, gentlemen, you know what your problems are; I do not need to elaborate. I am not here to enumerate your problems, I am here to introduce you to a method of solving them.

In my bag here, I have a fool proof method for controlling Black Slaves. I guarantee everyone of you that if installed correctly, it will control the slaves for at least 300 years. My method is simple and members of your family and any Overseer can use it.

I have outlined a number of difference(s) among the slaves; and I take these differences and make them bigger. I use fear, distrust, and envy for control purposes. These methods have worked on my modest plantation in the West Indies and [they] will work throughout the South. Take this simple little list of differences, think about them..On top of my list is "Age" but it is there only because it begins with an " A." The second is "Color" or "Shade," there is intelligence, size, sex, size of plantation, status of plantation, attitude of owner, whether the slaves live in the valley, on a hill, East, West, North, or South, have a fine or coarse hair, or is tall or short. Now that you have a list of differences, I shall give you an outline of action but before that, I shall assure you that distrust is stronger than trust and envy is stronger than adulation, respect and admiration.

The Black Slave, after receiving this indoctrination, shall carry on and will become self- refueling and self-generation for hundreds of years, maybe thousands.

Don't forget you must pitch the old black versus the young black and the young black male against the old black male. You must use the dark skin slave vs. the light skin slave and the light skin slaves vs. The dark skin slaves. You must also have your white servants and overseers distrust all blacks, but it is necessary that your slaves trust and depend on us. They must love, respect and trust only us.

Gentlemen, these Kits are keys to control, use them. Have your wives and children use them, never miss an opportunity. My plan is guaranteed and the good thing about this plan is that if used intensely for one year the slaves themselves will remain perpetually distrustful.

Thank you.*

Its creator guaranteed the above plan, and proponent to create division among slaves by focusing on differences and embellishing the differences to cause animosity and distrust that would last as a legacy through many descendants for hundreds of years. We can easily note slave masters and their agents carefully orchestrated the conflict and disunity that still exists between black men and women.

We can easily ascertain from the records the tortures the male slaves were subjected to, if they attempted to assert their African manliness. They quickly learned through a system of rewards and punishments that if they played the role expected they were rewarded. Is it any wonder that they portrayed "sambo" when it was expedient to do so? It is one thing to act a

---

* Willie Lynch's speech on his method for controlling slaves.

role, but quite another when the role develops into an automatic reaction within a given situation. How did this role-playing develop into psychological traits? With twenty-twenty hindsight we can now acquire an understanding of how the transformation process occurred.

Chapter 7

Negativisms Become Psychological Traits

Light was shed on this darkness when a Russian scientist while experimenting with dogs discovered "conditioning." Most school children have heard the name Pavlov. What made Pavlov a household name in psychology began as a study in digestion. He was observing the digestion process in dogs, especially the interaction between salivating and the activity of the stomach. He observed that reflexes in the nervous system linked them.Without salivation, the stomach didn't get the message to start digesting. Pavlov wanted to see if external stimuli could affect this process, so he rang a bell at the same time he gave food to the dogs in the experiment. After a while, the dogs -- which only salivated when they saw and ate their food -- started to salivate when the bell rang, even if no food was present. In 1903 Pavlov published the results of this experiment calling this a "conditioned reflex," different from an innate reflex, such as yanking a hand back from a flame, in that it had to be learned. Pavlov called this learning process (in which the dog's nervous system comes to associate the bell with the food, for example) "conditioning."

Just as the dog reacted in a particular manner when the bell (dynamic) was rung, thus associating the dynamic with food, and began to salivate, the male slave was given a choice of acting as expected and receives a reward. Acting contrary would invite torture or even death. After the first contrary act, or the witnessing of another slave receiving the tortuous punishment for his stance, the male slave usually complied with the master's expectations. Thus th e male slave "acted" the way expected by the master, and racism with its accompanying fear factor was the dynamics he associated with acting contrary to the master's wishes.

You might argue and dismiss this hindsight because it is based on the study of dogs. However, a South Carolinian, John Watson began observing infant humans and developed the science of behaviorism. Until then he had drawn comparisons between animals and humans, but hadn't experimented with them. His most famous experiment was conducted in the winter of 1919 and 1920 with a baby known as Albert. Watson and his assistant gave Albert a white lab rat, he was unafraid and tried to touch the rat. He was afraid, however, when they clanged metal with a hammer just behind his head, and he cried. A few months later, when Albert was 11 months old, they again gave him the rat, but this time just as he touched it, the metal clang sounded behind his head. That made him cry. This was repeated several times over a few weeks. Before long just the sight of the rat made Albert cry and try to crawl away.

This was the birth of "behaviorism," that branch of science that is based on the principle that thoughts, feelings, and intentions, all of which are mental processes, do not determine what we do. Our behavior is the product of our conditioning.

If indeed this is the case, then we can safely assume that it was within the crucible of slavery that the African American male's modern negative activities have their genesis. Our "Samboe" psychological traits[*] are continuing legacies, which are prompted out within the context of the same conditioning dynamics (racism[**]).

Noted psychiatrists, William H Greer, and Price M Cobbs confirm the assumption that the negative personality traits of the

---

[*] Compare to Ivan Pavlov's salivating dog & John Watson's crying baby.
[**] Ivan Pavlov's Bell & John Watson's Hammer.

African American Male has their origins in the Atlantic slave trade.

> The American black man is unique, but he has no special psychology or exceptional genetic determinants. His mental mechanisms are the same as other men. If he undergoes emotional conflict, he will respond as neurotically as his white brother. In understanding him we return to the same reference point, since all other explanations fail. We must conclude that much of the pathology we see in black people had its genesis in slavery. The culture that was born in that experience of bondage has been passed from generation to generation. Constricting adaptations developed during some long-ago time continue as contemporary character traits. That they are so little altered attests to the fixity of the black-white relationship, which has seen little change since the birth of this country.[62]

Subsequent generations of mostly black female mothers[*] have orally and by example, passed these traits down through her descendants. For instance, more than a few black mothers utilized physical beating of their children as a corrective and tool of control. Their daughters carried this practice into their families, and the continuing legacy goes on. Likewise, the negative traits developed by black men were passed on by them, generation after generation, passed on by way of imitation by black boys who use these males as role models, and these traits

---

[62] William H Grier and Price M Cobbs. *Black Rage*.N.Y:1968, Pp.30,31

[*] It was mostly, the mother who impacted on the child's behavior, rather than the father, because in many cases the male wasn't around often or long enough to influence much.

are re-enforced by the dynamics of racism. Many of these negative personality traits have been observed in practice even today, and recorded by many scholars.

To summarize, let me reiterate; African women once sat on thrones that ruled and provided civilization to the world, but currently occupy the lowest rungs in world social systems. They have fallen from the highest to the lowest because of disobedience to the God in whose image she is made,[*] and subsequently, for lack of sufficient protection and provisions by the African American males with whom they reproduce their future progeny.

If the African woman is to occupy her rightful throne again, African men must provide that throne, and protect it.

If we do not dare to struggle now, while we can still see a little light from what's left of day, the night and all of the fears and other unknown demons and denizens from hell will be upon us. Warped minds will do things under the cover of darkness, that can affect us in ways that further dehumanize us, or our complete elimination can be carried out in this lawless unknown. You may think the oppressor wouldn't do this, since you have developed a friendship with a member of the oppressor class. You have come to a place in your life where you just can't believe the oppressor has a program that will provide the final solution to the *problem*.

---

[*] Her own innately, peculiar self. Her Africa ness, which God created her to be. Her collectives self, which is connected through the ancestors, back to the beginning.

Chapter 8

The Final Solution

Extermination of the Black Race.

Albert Memmi, the Tunisian, Jewish freedom fighter believes the white oppressors in the United States, are in a process that leads inevitably to the extermination of the African American as the final solution to the problems they represent to them.

> As with most oppressions of one people by another, we discover here an inexorable process of systematic elimination. The fundamental desire of the white man, whether disguised or openly confessed, is to remove the black from his sight entirely. And, as Baldwin in this manifesto of his is staking his last chance, he follows his idea through to its conclusion: *in the final analysis what the white hopes for is the annihilation of the black.* Why the Americans should not one day attempt against their blacks what the Germans, another white, Christian nation, attempted against the Jews. Once again the reader is bound to protest when he reads this pitiless indictment. I believe, on the contrary, that Baldwin had glimpsed here a terrible truth: just as pogroms were no accident in Jewish history but the sign of an endemic disease, exacerbated and coming to a head, so lynchings,

> hangings and bonfires are the final explosion of the true sentiments of the white man with regard to the black man. [63]

Perhaps you may miss the import of the preceding belief of this Jewish intellect, but you cannot deny the millions of deaths during slavery, and the more than 5,000 known and recorded lynchings from slavery to today.

There appears to be an innate predisposition by Europeans to destroy the darker people of the world, Africans in particular. Black scholars have been searching for a clue to the motivating factor of their aggressiveness, and genocidal tendencies.

Genocide has been an operative solution to the problem of black people and other non-Europeans within the confines of the United States of America. This genocide is a conditioned reaction grounded in the Europeans' fear of the demise of their skin color and culture. This primal fear has been uncovered and defined by Doctor Frances Cress Welsing, in her revolutionary, groundbreaking, "Cress Theory of Color Confrontation."

> The Theory of Color-Confrontation states that the white or color-deficient Europeans responded psychologically with a profound sense of numerical inadequacy and color inferiority upon their confrontations with the massive majority of the world's people all of whom possessed varying degrees of color producing capacity. This psychological response, be it described as conscious or unconscious, was one of deeply sensed inadequacy which struck a blow at the

---

[63] Albert Memmi. *Dominated Man*. Boston:1968, p.23

> most obvious and fundamental part of their being, their external appearance.[64]

African Centered scholar, Marimba Ani, in her book, *Yurugu* finds the genesis of the problem is the power drive which is deeply embedded in and essential part of their cultural matrix which dictates to them to destroy the other.

> The motivating factor underlying European cultural aggression appears to be the power drive, which is fully acted out on the cultural other. This is often quite literally and dramatically the case; it is not merely a subtle implication of their cultural behavior. In 1816 a community of Africans, who had escaped from white slavers and who were living a quite peaceful, constructive, and culturally coherent existence in Florida, were attacked by a unit under the command of General Gaines of the United States Army; they were subsequently slaughtered.[65]

Marimba Ani also informs us of the opinion of an African American, trained in the field of medicine and specializing in surgery. She relates this doctor's belief that Aids target the colored races by design. The function of Aids is to decimate those groups considered a detrimental threat to white skin.

> Dr. Barbara Justice, a New York surgeon of African descent, believes: (I) The AIDS virus has been adapted to Melanin and is related to the

---

[64] Frances Cress Welsing. *The Cress theory Of Color Confrontation. The Black Scholar*. Vol. 5, Number 8. Sausalito: May 1974, p.34
[65] Marimba Ani. *Yurugu. An African Centered Critique of Europen Cultural Thought and Behavior*. Trenton: 1994, p.432

> experiment in 1951 with the death of a Diasporic African patient, Henrietta Lass, in which European scientists were able to grow viruses outside of the body in her cells after she had died: (2) The purpose of AIDS is to "clean out" the European gene pool, i.e., to eliminate "undesirables," Africans, and homosexuals; as well as to finally capture the continent of Africa by destroying its present, indigenous population. She refers us to the work of Jack Felder and Alan Cantwell, Jr.[66]

We cannot deny that evidence, and we cannot deny the Tuskegee experiment, or the Jamestown massacre, or the approximate, hundred millions murdered on the slave treks, in the forts, the bottom of the Atlantic ocean, on the plantations, and throughout the country, north, south, east, and west.

> The Guyanese Chief Medical Examiner testified in court that 80 percent of the bodies he examined showed signs of forcible injections. Jim Jones, the self-proclaimed leader of the "People's Temple" which moved to Guyana from San Francisco, and one of his aides, had CIA connections. The father of Jonestown leader Larry Layton was head of CBW Research at the Army's Dugway Proving Grounds in the 1950s. The elder Layton admitted contributing $25,000 to the People's Temple. According to Judge, "Public exposure [in the mid-1970s] of experiments in U.S. prisons and mental institutions was, in all likelihood, a major impetus

---

[66] Ibid. p.444

> for relocating this testing to the jungles of a virtually unknown country.[67]

Some scholars have advanced the theory of Aids being a biological weapon, and carried to its conclusion in its injections into the black citizens of various West African countries.

According to Robert Strecker, the Aids virus was manufactured in the United States and tested in West Africa.

> In our opinion, IARC, the International Agency for Research on Cancer, took these viruses to Africa in the early 1970s and tested them. Because we think they were trying to get the virus/cancer hypothesis proved; they wanted to develop a vaccine, and they wanted to find out which of those [viruses] were actually causing cancer because they weren't sure.[68]

Another instance of the oppressors disregards for the life of people of African descent, and the wantonly use of them as guinea pigs is noted in the following information.

> From 1956 to 1958, in the poor Black communities of Savannah, Georgia, and Avon Park, Florida, the Army carried out tests with mosquitoes that may have been infected with yellow fever. The insects were released into residential areas from ground level and dropped from planes and helicopters. Many people were

---

[67] Leonard G. Horowitz. *Emerging Viruses. Aids and Ebola*. MA:1966, p.322

[68] Leonard G. Horowitz. Emerging Viruses. Aids & Ebola. Nature, Accident or Intentional? Maine:1997, p.98.

swarmed by mosquitoes and then developed unknown fevers; some died. After each test Army agents posing as public health officials photographed and tested victims and then disappeared from town[69]

The following article from the New York Free Press, depicts a general underlying force that informs many white people of the United States of the final solution to black resistance against white oppression. That solution quite simply is, to annihilate the black man and woman, and eliminate the perpetual, problem at the same time.

This final solution is perhaps not so much a conspiracy, or for that matter a conscious plan to be executed, as it is a cultural and logical process that is progressive and more demanding as it works itself through to its inevitable conclusion. It starts as a belief in ones own superiority and its special privileges, as opposed to the other's inferiority and shortcomings, physically and spiritually.

NEW YORK PRESS
February 8, 1904

NEGRO AND WIFE BURNED

DODDSVILLE, Miss., Feb. 7-Luther Holbert and his wife, negroes, were burned at the stake here today by a mob of more than 1,000 persons for the killing of James Eastland, a prominent white planter, and John Carr, a negro, on Wednesday, at the Eastland plantation, two miles from this city. The burning of Holbert and his wife closes a

---

[69] ibid...p.322.

tragedy which has cost eight lives, has engaged 200 men and two packs of bloodhounds in a four days' chase across four Counties, and has stirred this section of Mississippi almost to frenzy. Following are the dead: Luther Holbert and wife, negroes, burned at the stake by mob; James Eastland, white, planter, killed by Holbert; john Carr, a negro, killed by Holbert; John Winters, negro, killed by Eastland, three unknown negroes, killed by posses. The killing of Eastland, Carr and Winters occurred Wednesday at Eastland's plantation. Holbert and Winters were in Carr's cabin when Eastland entered and ordered Holbert to leave the plantation. A difficulty ensued, in which it is alleged - that Holbert opened fire on Eastland, fatally wounding him and killing Carr. EasIand returned the fire and killed Winters.

When news of the tragedy reached Doddsville a posse was formed and left immediately for Eastland's plantation. Arriving there further shooting occurred, and an unknown negro was killed. Holbert and his wife had fled. Posses were formed at Greenville, Ittaben, Cleveland and other points and the pursuit of Holbert and his wife was begun with horses and bloodhounds. The chase, which was begun Wednesday morning, was continued until last night, when Holbert and wife, worn out from traveling over 100 miles on foot through canebrakes and swamps, were found asleep in a heavy belt of timber three miles east of Sheppardstown and captured. The two negroes were brought to Doddsville and this afternoon were burned at the stake by a large mob in the shadow of the negro church here.

Yesterday two negroes were killed by a posse near Belzoni, Yazoo County. One of the negroes bore a striking resemblance to Holbert, and was mistaken for him by members of the posse. Eastland was a member of a wealthy Mississippi family, and a reward of $1,200 was offered by relatives for the capture of his slayers. Two brothers of Eastland participated in the chase and capture of the Holberts and both were present when Holbert and his wife were burned.

The dead couple leaves a young son.

Let us not be lulled to sleep by the impotent pronouncements of the equality of man and, etc., however, let us always remember these are the same people who captured, bought, or kidnapped over 100,000,000 of our people and oppressed them in one of the worst holocausts to occur in recent history. This is the same people who methodically reduced our captured ancestors to less than human beings. They are the same ones who colonized America and practically annihilated the indigenous people. Yes, they are the same people who produced Hitler, and his Third Reich, which was directly responsible for annihilating over 6,000,000 Jews in Europe. This just so happens to be the same people responsible for the annihilation of millions upon millions of African people throughout the world. They are responsible for the annihilation of many individuals they considered as their enemies. The four girls in Birmingham, who fell victim to the blast from a bomb as they worshipped in church, as well as Malcolm X, ML King Jr., and the many thousands whom they hung on trees, or burned alive at the stakes. These are the same ones who decimated several black townships including the following.

> TULSA. On the last day of May, 1921 in Tulsa, Oklahoma, an African American named Rowland, was accused of attacking a white elevator girl. The white community armed itself for the lynching. African Americans armed themselves to prevent a lynching. There was a confrontation between the lynch mob and the black community, and the black community was able to hold the racist mob at bay until dawn the following day.
> It was on the following day, when the alleged culprit had already been removed from the city, that major violence occurred. Armed whites participated in a mass assault upon the Negro section, most of which was burned during-the rioting. Although heavy-armed resistance occasionally met the white attack, Negro activity was primarily defensive. Many fled the area and gave themselves up to white authorities. A Negro deputy sheriff was active in disarming many Negroes. What seems to have started as a result of the intention of some Negroes to prevent a possible lynching became, before its bloody conclusion, a massacre of Negroes reminiscent in character, if not in scale, of pogrom. Many People were killed, more Negroes than whites, and property damage in the Negro area amounted to almost total devastation of an area a mile square.[70]

---

[70] Allen Grimshaw. Racial Violence in the United States. Chicago:1969, p.107

We must help bring this white/racist/oppressive, madness to an end, because the future towards which white folks lead us is genocidal. We must use any and every means necessary and at our disposal to destroy it, or it will surely destroy us.

We must heed the call from famed poet Claude McKay in his poem, *If we must die*, to struggle against those who come to us operating within a determined program of genocide.

IF WE MUST DIE

IF we must die, let it not be like hogs
Hunted and penned in an inglorious spot,
While round us bark the mad and hungry dogs,
Making their mock at our accursed lot.
If we must die, O let us nobly die,
So that our precious blood may not be shed
In vain; then even the monsters we defy
Shall be constrained to honor us though dead!
O kinsmen! we must meet the common foe!
Though far outnumbered let us show us brave,
And for their thousand blows deal one deathblow!
What though before us lies the open grave?
Like men we'll face the murderous, cowardly pack,
Pressed to the wall, dying, but fighting back![71]

---

[71] Claude McKay. Selected Poems of Paul McKay.N.Y:1963, p.36

Part II
Restoration From Captivity
And Return To The Garden

Chapter 1

Reconciliation
Of Black Men and Women

If we as black people are to become liberated, there must first exist a unity amongst ourselves. This black unity is nothing more than unity between the black male and female. How can this unity be forged and made functional for our continuing struggle? The first step is for black men to repent* and seek black women's forgiveness for their irresponsible and destructive behavior in their relationship with them and the oppressors. The second step involves the black man's re-birth, and the black woman's complete confidence in him as her provider and protector.

Repentance is the state of being you have reached through an understanding that what you have done is wrong, and you evidence remorse and seek forgiveness from, and reconciliation with the one wronged. We have wronged our black queens. We have reduced them from our queens to "hoes" and "bitches,"* as the current rap generation illustrate in their modern music. We must begin to elevate the black woman to her original role and importance in our lives. We must remove the veil covering our seeing eye and observe the black queen in all of her beautiful splendor. She must be observed as the "Queen of Heaven,"

---

* Come to a place in our lives where we realize and acknowledge that what we have been doing is wrong, and then cease from doing it.

* These are terms usually associated with, promiscuous human females, and female dogs.

and mother of mankind. She must be seen as one of the most beautiful creatures to ever stroll the planet earth. She must be seen as a prize worth suffering for, and if necessary, dying for. She must be defined this way because that's what she really is.

Before the black man can see the black woman in a positive light, however, he must first see himself in a positive light. In order for this to occur, he should engage in struggle, and make conscious efforts through a deliberate and proper, independent education to de-brainwash himself. This is the case because a transformation in the mind leads to a corresponding transformation in action. The black man's mind was transformed during slavery and must be re-transformed if he is to become himself. We are all in a state of becoming, but what we shall become is determined to a large extent by ourselves and through the choices we make.

However, our choices are determined in an atmosphere of threatened pain and rewards. If we make the choice to struggle in the streets, we are attacked and killed. On the individual level, if we become too radical we are isolated and destroyed by whatever means, and on whatever level. On the other hand we are rewarded if we acquiesce and accommodate ourselves to our prescribed, oppressed condition. So, you see we are in a no win situation in our choice of being oppressed or not if we are looking for an easy way out. We can and must make our choice to be liberated beings. I say our choice because it is evident to me that there can be no oppressor unless someone makes the choice to become the oppressed. The oppressed makes his choices in an atmosphere of fear. It is this fear that controls him. If he is to overcome his fears he must face them. Quite simply, our source of fear is the white oppressor, and in order for us to overcome it, we must face the white oppressor.

Of course, the oppressors will react to our bold stand with violence. We have been the recipients of his violence for over 500 years. What else is new? The only thing he can do is escalate his violence, but he cannot force us to make a particular choice. There was violence in the capture of our ancestors. There was violence used in their forced transit across the Atlantic. There was widespread violence on the plantations. There was violence after chattel slavery, in the lynchings that took place throughout the country. Today there is violence in the injustices of the educational, judicial, political, social, and economic systems. However, even as a target for all of the violence and threats of the system, the black man still has the power to make his choices himself. That power resides in each and every individual that inhabits God's earth. Nothing can take that power away, however, it can be given away. The way we give it away is when we make choices opposed to the ones we want to make, because of fear of definite, or implied outside threats.

We must begin to make the correct choices if we are to find reconciliation with our black women. Since we are in a state of total oppression, we have a difficult task of re-defining ourselves in the midst of a system whose information media, educational, judicial, political, and social components reinforce the oppressor's definition of who and what we are. Consequently, we must engage the total system if we are to have a real opportunity for liberation, and reconciliation with our queens.

During our engagement with the system, we must consciously, and continuously re-define ourselves, and make a willed effort to evidence that newly defined self in our relationships with the oppressors, and amongst ourselves. In our re-definition of ourselves, concomitantly, we re-define the oppressor. When we lift ourselves up, we also pull down the foundation that supports the concept of the superiority of the oppressors.

While defining ourselves in the midst of struggle, we must drop to our knees, and implore black women to forgive us for not being there for them as self-dependant, protectors and providers. We must make a holy pledge with them, to love and support one another until the end of times. We must shower them with the praises that are due them. We must impress on them their importance to us as the means by which we reproduce ourselves. We must begin to understand that when we denigrate the black woman and lower her esteem to that of a garbage can, that we are in actuality consigning our future generation's self-esteem to the equivalence of garbage. Remember garbage comes out of garbage cans, and queens produce princesses. We must bring this cyclical problem to a halt, and elevate the black woman to her rightful place in the world. She is its unmitigated queen. When we stand up like the potential men we are, and shower our love and respect on the black woman, she likewise, will forgive us, and reflect that love and respect back to us.

We can only lift the Black woman as high as we assume we are. Let me explain. If I hate myself, I can't love the Black woman. If I believe I am an inferior being, then correspondingly, I most likely will view the black woman as also inferior. Consequently, in order for Black men to lift Black women up, they must also lift themselves up. How do Black men lift themselves up? This is a task where each individual lifts the other up, and then that one enhances the up lifting of another and so on. Or, as is commonly stated, "each one should help one."

What is it each one can help each one with? We can help one another by constantly reminding each other of who we really are. Who are we? We are first of all, representatives of the first man God created. In other words God created the Black man. All other groups descended from the Black man. We are the creators of the world's first and grandest civilizations, and by many migrations from Africa spread civilization to the world. We have been in decline for several thousand years, but our impress on the world is still rather profound. My contention is, whatever we were, we still are, more or less. Our suppressed greatness and influence is still there, and others know and benefit from it. This is evidenced in the constantly, imitating, and confiscation of our creations.

Examples:
1. I can remember a time when white people and many black people considered it uncouth to wear a cap, or hat backwards on your head. However, some black men did wear their hats and caps backwards in spite of the values of many Blacks and Whites. Of course, they were looked down on by Black people because they thought it made the race look bad. They were looked down on by many White people as being anti-social, "niggers." But, if you take note, our Black youth began wearing their caps backwards during the Hip-Hop revolution, and almost every kid and many adults, black, white and in between are imitating our kids and wearing their caps backwards.
2. I visited Japan in 1954, and like most servicemen became a regular visitor to the various clubs around Tokyo. The motivation for my frequent club hopping was the Japanese jazz musicians, and singers who were excellent technicians, and imitators of Black jazz musicians. You would have thought you were in New York, listening to, and enjoying music by black jazz bands.
3. In 1956, I visited the Philippine Islands for two years. During my stay there I was impressed with the entire country's love of the Platters, and other black soul groups. The younger people were engrossed in this

music. Their young people imitated these groups, especially, the R& B group, the *Platters*.

Many of us may find the language and images used by Rappers as appalling, but our youth have the world in their hands on this one, and have many people throughout the world, adopting their style, and utilizing their form of speech and symbols, in imitation of them.

4. The majority of the world's population uses all of our musical forms, and some exploiters have made millions of dollars off our creations. There is a plethora of white rappers, imitating our youth.

Imitation is the highest form of flattery. It is rather ironic, the man who is supposedly, the lowest of human kind, is the most imitated being on the planet. White males often try to walk like them, talk like them, sing like them, and most of all, be like them.

It has been shown by scientific evidence that the early Egyptians, Babylonians, Sumerians, so-called East Indians, and others were Africans (Hamites, Cushites, Ethiopians, etc.). Yet, misled, or racist scholars insist in the face of convincing scientific evidence, that these ancient civilizations were originated by an imaginary Caucasian brown race, originating in the proximity of the Mediterranean.

The only reason we haven't excelled in other areas, other than sports and entertainment, is because we are prevented from competing in them. We must be kept out, or we would excel and take over. The oppressor knows what you are capable of, only you, the oppressed are still in the dark. Wake up, mighty black man, and recognize who you are. You are the crown of God's creation, so begin to act like it. Begin immediately to see and believe you are the king of the world. You have merely abdicated your throne, by submitting to the will of the outside other. Listen to that most ancient spirit within, and let it guide you to your rightful throne, and seat yourself besides your beautiful, and strong, black queen.

This kingdom we are to re-create will be physical as well as spiritual. However, in both aspects of the kingdom we must provide protection, and sustenance for one another.

It is difficult to protect and provide for the black woman, if we do not have the necessary defensive resources. We are in a state of war with those whose interest it is to keep us in conflict and divided. In war you must be able to defend yourself. These defensive resources are: control of a food supply, shelter, defensive weapons, capital, and land that we control. With these resources we would have for the first time in approximately 500 years, the necessities required for the elevation, and protection of the black woman's esteem, and our national liberation.

The lack of a political land base has been a main contributor to our weaknesses. We have had to depend on others for our basic needs. What happens when your suppliers become your enemies? They can stop your supplies, or poison your food, or whatever they determine. Malcolm X, consistently reminded us, "in the final analysis, all revolution is fought over the question of land." Land offers political and economic freedom. Do we want to stay in this current oppressed, dependant situation? No, we need to become politically and economically free, and develop ourselves into the protectors and providers for black women, and our people, as God created us to become. In order to be successful in this endeavor, we must occupy our own land.

Chapter 2

A New Garden of Eden
To Rule And Exploit

Let us begin with where most of our people reside spiritually. To do this, our point of departure must be the Christian Bible. If we hope to reach, and inform that segment from which the determination to do what is necessary to bring about our liberation, we must meet them where they are. First, they have to be made aware that God ordains their liberation from all that binds and oppress them.

In the biblical paradigm[72] of the reported slave exodus from Egypt, which we have traditionally used as our model for liberation, we must note that God not only promised to provide freedom and reparations to the oppressed Hebrews, but He also earlier promised to their reported father, Abraham, some land.

> And I will give this people favor in the sight of the Egyptians; and it shall come to pass, that, when you go, ye shall not go empty But every woman shall borrow of her neighbour, and of her that sojourn in her house, jewels of silver, and jewels of gold, and raiment: and ye shall put them upon your sons, and upon your daughters; and ye shall spoil the Egyptians.[73]

---

[72] See; John D Brinson. *Reparations! And God's Judgment*. Richmond:2002
[73] Ex. 3:21,22

He promised them the land of Canaan, as a homeland, which would provide for their national defense, and solidify their political and economic liberation. Here is God's promise to Abraham.

> 12 As the sun was setting, Abram fell into a deep sleep, and a thick and dreadful darkness came over him. 13 Then the LORD said to him, "Know for certain that your descendants will be strangers in a country not their own, and they will be enslaved and mistreated four hundred years. 14 But I will punish the nation they serve as slaves, and afterward they will come out with great possessions. 15 You, however, will go to your fathers in peace and be buried at a good old age. 16 In the fourth generation your descendants will come back here, for the sin of the Amorites has not yet reached its full' measure. " 17 When the sun had set and darkness had fallen, a smoking firepot with a blazing torch appeared and passed between the pieces. 18 On that day the LORD made a covenant with Abram and said, "To your descendants I give this land, from the river of Egypt to the great river, the Euphrates - 19 the land of the Kenites, Kenizzites, Kadmonites, 20 Hittites, Perizzites, Rephaites, Amorites, Canaanites, Girgashites and Jebusites."[74]

However, they remained in the wilderness until they were forged into a cultural and military nation, afterwards they conquered the Canaanites, and took their land. It must be noted

---

[74] Genesis 15:12-21

that to give birth to the new nation required the use of violence to conquer and secure the land. It was a most violent conquest.

> 21 At that time Joshua went and destroyed the Anakites from the hill country: from Hebron, Debir and Anab, from all the hill country of Judah, and from all the hill country of Israel. Joshua totally destroyed them and their towns. 22 No Anakites were left in Israelite territory; only in Gaza, Gath and Ashdod did any survive. 23 So Joshua took the entire land, just as the LORD had directed Moses, and he gave it as an inheritance to Israel according to their tribal divisions.
> Then the land had rest from war.[75]

God, as portrayed in the Christian religion is not a respecter of persons. He is the God who intervenes on the side of the downtrodden and oppressed, and always fights their battles. because He is righteous, and it is the righteous thing to do.

We must begin the struggle for the land. It will more likely than not, be a very tough struggle. But, hasn't all our struggling to survive and rise in the midst of total oppression, been a tough and difficult struggle? One fact we need to keep in the forefront of our minds is that the outcome of the struggle will depend to a large extent upon the condition of our minds. Our minds have been conditioned to have no faith in our own ability, but to believe the oppressor is capable of accomplishing anything. This precept must be rejected and destroyed. The script must be flipped. We must believe in our own ability to accomplish anything we focus on, and dedicate ourselves to; and the oppressor and his forces incapability of stopping us. One

---

[75] Joshua 11:21-23

African American scholar, claims we must begin to think about struggling for land to own and its control.

> What is more, the struggle can be successful. A great deal, however, depends upon how fast and how completely Africans in America can un-track their minds from the inability to think about land, independent land, as not only an integral part of our struggle for freedom but as an essential primary goal. For success of the struggle depends a great deal upon the support which those of us who now opt for and are working to build an independent African nation on this soil, get from those of us who do not now choose for themselves the route of an independent nation. (We calculate that those who do not now opt for independence may number as many as two-fifths of our people.) And the support of these people must be founded upon an understanding of what the New Africans are about.
> Perhaps the best way for people to untrack their minds from the slaving inability to think of land as a real and legitimate goal of our struggle is to understand how a people acquire claim to land. There is, of course, what we call the bandit rule of international law; this says, essentially, that if a people steals land and occupies it for a long time, the world will recognize that land as belonging to them. This, of course, is the manner in which the United States acquired claim to most of America: white folks simply stole it and held it. As a people we Africans in America have been cowed by this rule; we have cringed before it (and before the

power of the beast) as if it were the only rule of land possession.[76]

The provider of the following information, Mr. Haki R Madhubuti in the following quotation, notes also for us, the importance of a politically controlled territory, or land as it is generally referred to.

> Land is all important. Land is the only thing that nobody, nowhere, is making any more of. We can buy the cars next year, buy the latest horse wigs anytime, but land is going fast and white people are aware of this because they are all over the world trying to control the *land.* Land is the substance of life. We can't grow food on all this concrete. We are moving into the twenty first century and southern Afrika is still not liberated. It is highly contradictory for this country, other western powers, the western church and the U.N. to talk about individual freedom and inalienable rights of man while they *covertly* and overtly aid the existence of white settlers in southern Afrika. Azania (South Afrika), Namibia, Botswana and Zimbabwe (Rhodesia) are not controlled by the majority who are black people. These areas are controlled by white settlers who have no legal, historical or cultural ties to Afrika.[77]

Highly respected and world renowned, African American scholar, WEB Dubois informs us of the desire for land by our

---

[76] Imari Abubakari Obadele. *Foundation of the Black Nation*. San Francisco: 1975, Pp.2, 3.
[77] Haki R. Madhubuti. Enemies. *The Clash of the Races*. Chicago:1978, p.99

ex-slave, ancestors and their support from some members of the white government. Thaddeus Stevens and Charles Sumner both recognized the economic importance land would play in the lives of our so-called freed ancestors, and tried to convince the government to provide some land for them. But their will and desires could not come into fruition while the racists and economic interests of the country were vigorously trying to destroy the possibility of land reform.

> Again and again, crudely but logically, the Negroes expressed their right to the land and the deep importance of this right. And as usual here the government played fast and loose because it had two irreconcilable ideas in mind. Thaddeus Stevens and Charles Sumner were perfectly clear; the Negroes must have land furnished them either for a nominal sum or as a gift, and this land should be furnished by the government and paid for either out of taxation, or as Stevens repeatedly insisted, as an indemnity placed on the South for civil war. Moreover, for 250 years the Negroes had worked on this land, and by every analogy in history, when they were emancipated the land ought to have belonged in large part to the workers.[78]

He also advises us that many intellectuals did not take the desire for land as serious. The oppressor understands to clearly that control of land translates into economic and political freedom. Your freedom would mean his profits are to decrease.

---

[78] WEB Dubois. *Black Reconstruction*. New York:1935, p.368.

> Most writers, and speakers thought of the land problem so far as the Negro was concerned as an incidental thing; it was something that "would come." On the other hand, the former slaveholders knew that land was the key to the situation and they tried desperately to center thought on labor rather than on land ownership. " One universal opinion is that they shall not be allowed to acquire or hold land. I have heard that expressed from the first. They say that unless Negroes work for them they shall not work at all.[79]

The question of the land must be seriously taken into account! There is no revolution without the confiscation of, and redistribution of the land. Revolution is ultimately, always about the land, which provides protection and basic resources.

After the civil war, blacks indicated their knowledge of how important land was in freedom by struggling with whites for ownership, and control of it.

> In the first year of freedom former slaves manifested an extraordinary determination to acquire land. Clearly land ownership was next to freedom itself as a priority. Some of the blacks settled in nearby pinelands, such as the Free Woods, where they could purchase land for a dollar an acre and could pay for it with rice. Others lay claim to the plantations on which they had spent their working lives. Many of the white planters had abandoned their Waccamaw plantations for inland safety during the war, leaving their slaves behind to work the land. In

---

[79] Ibid, p.369

1865 those slaves, now free, believed that the land and the crops should remain In their hands. The Freedmen's Bureau Act of March 3, 1865, authorized freed men to preempt forty acres of abandoned or confiscated land at 'minimal rent for three years and to buy it for a fairly appraised price. Blacks thus had to occupy the land in order to gain it; whites had to occupy the land in order to retain it. Tension was inevitable; the closest former slaves and former masters came to armed conflict over this question. In this contest the white planters ultimately prevailed, not because of any lack of will on the part of the freedmen, but because of the willingness of Federal authorities to sustain the planters' legal claim to the land.[80]

We must return to the basic understanding our ancestors had concerning the connection between freedom and the land. Without political ownership of our own sovereign piece of dirt, we will always be dependent on the owners of the land of our captivity for its resources, and we may forever remain defenseless in face of those who come after us operating from a mode of genocide. Let's us begin the struggle for the land before it is too late.

---

[80] Charles Joyner. *Down By The Riverside. A South Carolina Slave Community*. Chicago:1985. Pp.234-235.

Chapter 3

Total Revolt

There are only two choices for the oppressed being; he can accommodate himself to the situation, or he can revolt against it. In spite of what some theorist propound, the oppressed has only two choices. It is either freedom, or oppression. If he is to be free, he must resign himself to total revolt, for there is in reality no other road that leads to liberation from total domination.

> To sum up, if we define total oppression as a state which affects the human being in all aspects of his existence, in the way he sees himself and the way others see him, in his various entrees into urban society, and his future in history, then the oppression of the American Negro is undeniably a total oppression. A product of the whole of American society, it affects the whole of the black man's existence.[81]

Consequently, the only avenue that leads towards freedom is found in the process of total revolt. Quite literally, this means revolt against every aspect of this racist, oppressive system. Total revolt dawns when those who are oppressed have their

---

[81] Albert Memmi. *Dominated Man.* Boston: 1968, Pp.22, 23.

backs against the wall, and feel they have nothing to lose and everything to gain. This means war and the planned implementation of violence without rules. There is no compromise in total revolt, because its very being predisposes a goal of the reversal of the order and nature of the context in which the total oppression occurs. Or, as it is commonly stated, "the last shall be first, and the first shall be last."

> ... if the last shall be first, this will only come to pass after a murderous and decisive struggle between the two protagonists. That affirmed intention to place the last at the head of things, and to make them climb at a pace (too quickly, some say) the well-known steps which characterize an organized society, can only triumph if we use all means to turn the scale, including, of course, that of violence.[82]

Because we focused on a narrow aspect of our oppression, the all-pervasive tentacles of oppression undermined the theoretical gains that were provided us. We must not succumb to the quick fix, or the path of least resistance in our thrust for liberation in the future. The oppressors have too much to lose, and they will utilize any, and all strategies and tactics to keep control, and special privileges. The oppressors must be overthrown and replaced if the revolt is to lead to liberation. How else can the dominated be free of domination unless that which dominates is overthrown? It will be a time of clearing of the psyche of slavery and its current psychological legacies. It shall be like a chaotic storm clearing the air of all past determining dynamics. Total revolt is the state where all the resources of defense and offense of the oppressed and oppressor

---

[82] Frantz Fanon. *The Wretched of the Earth*. New York:1963, p.37

meet with the understanding and determination that when the smoke clears only one of the forces shall remain.

The following example of total revolt is a quotation from CLR James, and is based on the total revolt of the slaves against the masters in the Caribbeans, during the Atlantic Slave Trade.

> The slaves destroyed tirelessly. Like the peasants in the Jacquerie or the Luddite wreckers, they were seeking their salvation in the most obvious way, the destruction of what they knew was the cause of their sufferings; and if they destroyed much it was because they had suffered much. They knew that as long as these plantations stood their lot would be to labour on them until they dropped. The only thing was to destroy them. From their masters they had known rape, torture, degradation, and, at the slightest provocation, death. They returned in kind. For two centuries the higher civilisation had shown them that power was used for wreaking your will on those whom you controlled. Now that they held power they did as they had been taught. In the frenzy of the first encounters they killed all, yet they spared the priests whom they feared and the surgeons who had been kind to them. They, whose women had undergone countless violations, violated all the women who fell into their hands, often on the bodies of their still bleeding husbands, fathers and brothers. "Vengeance! Vengeance!" was their war-cry, and one of them carried a white child on a pike as a standard.[83]

---

[83] CLR James. The Black Jacobins. New York::1962 ,p.88

As cruel and dehumanizing as it is, total revolt, ultimately means revolt against, and destruction of everything associated with the oppressors. The goal of total revolt is to make "the last first, and the first, last. There is no way yet known by men by which the world can be turned topsy-turvy without the intervention of violence. The very thought and discussion of total revolt conjures up total violence. Total revolt and total violence are but different sides of the same coin. You can't have one without the other.

Chapter 4

Old Testament Violence

In the Old Testament's tradition on the account of the twelve tribe's struggle to conquer the land of Canaan, we are led to believe that many thousands of the indigenous people were violently removed from the land. A few of those scriptures that relates the same, follows for your perusal and edification.

> *Num.* 31: 7. And they warred against the Midianites, as the LORD commanded Moses; and they slew all the males.
> - - -8. And they slew the kings of Midian, beside the rest of them that were slain; namely, Evi, and Rekem, and Zur, and Hur, and Reba, five kings of Midian: Balaam also the son of Beor they slew with the sword.
> *Jud.* 1: 4. And Judah went up; and the LORD delivered the Canaanites and the Perizzites into their hand: and they slew of them in Bezek ten thousand men.
> ---10. And Judah went against the Canaanites that dwelt in Hebron: now the name of Hebron before was Kirjath-arba: and they slew Sheshai, and Ahiman, and Talmai.
> --- 7: 25. And they took two princes of the Midianites, Oreb and Zeeb; and they slew Oreb upon the rock Oreb, and Zeeb they slew at the

winepress of Zeeb, and pursued Midian, and brought the heads of Oreb and Zeeb to Gideon on the other side Jordan.
---8: 10. Now Zebah and Zalmunna were in Karkor, and their hosts with them, about fifteen thousand men, all that were left of all the hosts of the children of the east: for there fell a hundred and twenty thousand men that drew sword.
1Chr. 18:5 And when the Syrians of Damascus came to help Hadarezer king of Zobah, David slew of the Syrians two and twenty thousand men.
---12. Moreover, Ablshai the son of Zeruiah slew of the Edomites in the valley of salt eighteen thousand.
2 *Sam.* 10: 18. And the Syrians fled before Israel; and David slew the men of seven hundred chariots of the Syrians, and forty thousand horsemen, and smote Shobach the captain of their host, who died there.
1 *Chr.* xix. 18. But the Syrians fled before Israel; and David slew of the Syrians seven thousand men which fought in chariots, and forty thousand footmen, and killed Shophach the captain of the host.
1 *Kings* xx. 29. And they pitched one over against the other seven days. And *so* it was, that in the seventh day the battle was joined: and the children of Israel slew of the Syrians a hundred thousand footmen in one day.

Not only were the original inhabitants of the land violently eliminated, but also on several occasions violence reached its zenith, when the towns they occupied were burned to oblivion. Below are a few scriptures that indicate this to be the case.

Captured Cities Burned.

Deut. 13: 16. And thou shalt gather all the spoil of it into the midst of the street thereof, and shalt burn with fire the city, and all the spoil thereof every whit, for the LORD thy God: and it shall be a heap forever; it shall not be built again.

Num. 21: 28. For there is a fire gone out of Heshbon, a flame from the city of Sihon: it hath consumed Ar of Moab, and the lords of the high places of Amon.

---31: 10. And they burnt all their cities wherein they dwelt, and all their goodly castles, with fire.

Jud. 1: 8. Now the children of Judah had fought against Jerusalem, and had taken it, and smitten it with the edge of the sword, and set the city on fire.

---9: 48. And Abimelech gat him up to mount Zalmon, he and all the people that were with him; and Abimelech took an axe in his hand, and cut down a bough from the trees, and took it, and laid *it* on his shoulder, and said unto the people that were with him, What ye have seen me do, make haste, and do as I have done.

---49. And all the people likewise cut down every man his bough, and followed Abimelech, and put them to the hold, and set the hold on fire upon them; so that all the men of the tower of Shechem died also, about a thousand men and women.

---20: 48. And the men of Israel turned again upon the children of Benjamin, and smote them with the edge of the sword, as well the men of every city, as the beast, and all that came to hand: also they set on fire all the cities that they came to.

The reason for the pointing to the use of violence by the folk of the Old Testament is to showcase its inevitable place in the process for peoples' liberation, and not as an act of condonement. Just as the twelve tribes were engulfed in violence as they struggled to liberate, and gain control of the land, the black liberator, and white oppressor must drench the soil in their own blood if the hope for liberation is to become a tangible reality.

Chapter 5

Violence and Jesus

We must remember Jesus utilized an extreme method when he turned over the tables in the temple, and drove out the various temple polluters, by whipping them with twisted cords. His claim for His actions was as follows.

> 13. When it was almost time for the Jewish Passover, Jesus went up to Jerusalem. 14. In the temple courts he found men selling cattle, sheep and doves, and others sitting at tables exchanging money. 15.So he made a whip out of cords, and drove all from the *temple* area, both sheep and cattle; he scattered the coins of the money changers and overturned their tables. 16. To those who sold doves he said, "Get these out of here! How dare you turn my Father's house into a market! [84]

Jesus used violence to clear the temple of desecrations and the desecrators, because God's place of spiritual habitation must be kept holy. It might be interesting to point out that the Bible plainly teaches on the inhabitation of the temple* of believers

---

[84] John 2:13-16, NIV
* The believer's body is the temple of God.

by the Spirit of God[85]. If this is the case, then we should emulate Jesus, and use whatever means it takes to keep his temple holy from all pollutions and polluters.

Christ's disciple, Peter was representative of the rock of faith on which Jesus announced, "Upon this rock, I will build my church.," but we are informed that Peter carried a sword, and didn't hesitate to use it when he thought it necessary. When Jesus fell into the hands of his enemies, and was arrested, Peter came to his defense, withdrew his sword, and severed one of the enemy's ears.

> 50 Jesus replied, "friend, do what you came for." Then the men stepped forward, seized Jesus and arrested him. 51 With that, one of Jesus' companions reached for his sword, drew it out and struck the servant of the high priest, cutting off his ear.[86]

But, Jesus immediately ordered him to put his sword up, and cease from violence. Then Jesus explains why violence shouldn't be used. If you use violence, the Romans will retaliate with a greater violence, and you will die. Besides, you can't do anything to change the unfolding events that points towards Calvary. It must happen this way so Scripture can be fulfilled.

> Put your sword back in its place," Jesus said to him, "for all who draw the sword will die by the sword. Do you think I cannot call on my Father, and he will at once put at my disposal more than twelve legions of angels? But how then can the

---

[85] See 1Cor.3:16,17
[86] Matt. 26:50,51

Scripture be fulfilled that say it must happen in this way?"[87]

Jesus reminded his disciple, that his kingdom is not necessarily political but spiritual in nature. Consequently, there is no need for the sword, because violence begets violence, and if he had needed a political victory, he could have called "twelve legions of angels" for his disposal of the enemy. Jesus advised him things had to be this way so that his suffering, required by prophecy, might be fulfilled.

---

[87] Matt. 26:52-54.

Chapter 6

Violence At Calvary

When we turn our attention to the drama at Calvary, we can note it was a most violent act. The Bible text informs us that Christ was beaten and scourged while struggling uphill towards Calvary, with the heavy load of the cross on his back. I would classify this as violent assaults against His person. The text further informs us, that spikes were driven through both his hands and feet, and a spear was thrust into his side. Afterwards He hung His head and died. You must admit the Christ suffered a painful and violent death. The cost of our redemption, and reconciliation was the violently shed blood of the Christ. Redemption requires the shedding of blood. Christian believers receive that redemption after securing coverage under the shed blood of the Christ.

> And almost all things are by the law purged with blood; and without shedding of blood is no remission.[88]

Calvary is the place where the liberation from oppression is absolved in blood, and oppression comes to an end. Calvary is the place where death, and the possibility of a new life are exposed. Calvary is the experience after all, which makes Easter possible. Consequently, Calvary is the place where oppressor

---

[88] Hebrews 9:22

and the victim must meet if redemption, reconciliation, and resurrection of the "new creature" are to be experienced.

The guilty ones have already been sentenced by the Lord, in that they were told, "the wages of sin is death." Without finding redemption and reconciliation, they must pay the price themselves for the brokenness and separation their actions caused in their victims. Blood is the only remission for sin. You either pay with your blood, or a surrogate must pay for you.

History indicates that the dominated will inevitably move towards violence as they struggle for liberation, and the process towards liberation advances. I am not advocating violence, but rather, I am merely recognizing, and acknowledging a stage in the process towards liberation. This process can be noted during our historical levels of struggle against that which dominates us. This process can be discerned in the persona, actions and goals of Martin Luther King, and Malcolm X.[89] You see, Martin and Malcolm were really surrogates for the process that is occurring within the Black man and woman's psychic. That process is as follows. We have gone through the first stage of the oppressed, identification with and hope in the oppressors, the adoption of his values, and an attempt to become integrated. M.L. King Jr is the personification of this stage. The second stage is total rejection of the oppressor, and the escalation of violence as a tool for liberation. Malcolm X personifies this stage. Albert Memmi succinctly describes this phenomenon.

> In actual fact, King and Malcolm draw on two myths, or two counter-myths born out of the affliction of the black American. Both of them demand freedom and dignity for their people, but they each translate in their own way one or another of the answers that the down-trodden

---

[89] This is a clear model of WEB Dubois' "Double consciousness" concept.

black can give his oppressor. King hopes to disarm the whites by a great act of love, repeated over and over until the two races fuse and become one. There is nothing absurd in this so long as there remains a hope that the white man will finally consent to this love. In the meantime, King's patience and his dreams certainly help to pass the time of waiting. But how can one ever expect the oppressor's consent, when in the contract that seals their union he must sign away his privileges? Even without taking into account the horror for white Americans of having to abandon the image they have created of themselves and of America. Historically speaking, nights like the fourth of August in France are rare, or else mere illusions. It is not often that they can prevent the victim from discovering that his patience is in vain, or hinder the revolt from taking its course. Malcolm is purely the embodiment of this intuition, on the verge of despair, that all is useless; *rev*olt is first of all the acknowledgment of an impossible situation.[90]

You might say and be correct, Martin Luther King, and Malcolm X, represent two consciousnesses of African Americans. Both of which have their origin in slavery. They have their genesis in, and flow from the myth of "house slave," and "field slave."

We must remember, when we struggle against oppression, we do not bring violence, but rather, violence is an integral part of oppression. When confronted, the perpetual violence of the system is escalated and becomes evident for the masses to

---

[90] Albert Memmi. *Dominated Man*.Boston:1968, Pp.14,15.

witness and suffer from. The masses will then use defensive violence to end the oppressor's violence. All oppressive systems are created by and maintained by violence. Frantz Fanon makes the following observation.

> Their first encounter was marked by violence and their existence together - that is to say the exploitation of the native by the settler-was carried on by dint of a great array of bayonets and cannons. The settler and the native are old acquaintances. In fact, the settler is right when he speaks of knowing "them" well. For it is the settler who has brought the native into existence and who perpetuates his existence. The settler owes the fact of his very existence, that is to say, his property, to the colonial system.[91]

Violence is initiated by, and is perpetuated by the oppressors, and when the oppressed resist their oppression, they become the recipients of that violence. However, it is a God given mandate for humans to resist oppression of all kinds. Consequently, we must resist at any cost.

The following statement is the last recorded statement given by a son of the oppressors, before he was executed for engaging the government in struggle to liberate our slave ancestors. His statement agrees with the one made by Thomas Jefferson in his belief that this country of oppressors had to pay the inevitable, price in blood when the time comes. Here is John Brown's last statement.

> I, John Brown, am not quite certain that the crimes of this guilty land will ever be purged away but

---

[91] Frantz Fanon. *Wretched of the Earth*. New York: 1963

with blood. I had, as I now think vainly, flattered myself that without very much bloodshed it might be done.[92]

Violence appears to be the only language the oppressor understands, and consequently, we must speak to him in such a manner that he understands, liberation will be ours or he shall reap the judgment of fire.

What good function can violence serve? First, let me say that acts of violence are appalling, but whether the country is to become drenched in blood is not my decision. Like anyone else, I dread that awful day, but it is up to the oppressors whether the struggle advances to that stage. But, violence clears the air; it acts as a catharsis in bringing about release of the accumulated repressed anger and feeling of helplessness. It purges the psyche of fear, which has been the historical tool of control in oppression. You might say and be correct, revolutionary violence can be a liberator of the mind, and emotions.

Liberation is always a violent phenomenon. History illustrates for us that without violence, there is no liberation, there is only at best, noise from uncoordinated blaring of horns, and the clanging of cymbals, which means absolutely nothing. It is rather, a trick utilized to make you think you hear beautiful music. But, when the band stops and you reflect on what you thought you were receiving, you realize you were had again. You thought for a while you heard music, but suddenly realized that wasn't music, it was just noise.

Liberation brings about disorder, as its goal is to change the order of the system from top to bottom. The struggle for liberation brings into violent conflict two diametrically opposed

---

[92] As recorded in; Joanne Grant. *Black Protest. History, Documents, and analyses. 1619 to the Present*. Connecticut:1968, P. 83.

forces, the oppressed and the oppressor. The dominated man "finds his freedom in and through violence."[93]

We were taught in school, that Abraham Lincoln, the "great emancipator" of the oppressed slave, proclaimed in his First Inaugural Address:

> This country, with its institutions, belongs to the people who inhabit it. Whenever they shall grow weary, of the existing government, they can exercise their constitutional right of amending it, or their revolutionary right to dismember, or overthrow it.

According to old Abe, people have a revolutionary right to overthrow the government, which has, or has allowed others to torture and kill them to the point of their over weariness. The only way the oppressed can end their oppressive weariness, is to neutralize the source of their weariness.

It took the blood of Christ to provide the absolution of the guilt of sinners, and reconcile them to the Father. It will likewise take the shedding of blood in the United States, to absolve the oppressor of his sin, and guilt, and reconcile him to the oppressed Blacks whom he has sinned against. That's the way it was, is, and perhaps, always will be. The oppressors must bear the cross, which stands as a testament and revelation to, and of a love that bears all, without any resentment whatsoever. This is the road they must of necessity, travel if they are to clear their conscience of guilt and become reconciled to their victims. When the time comes, and it most certainly shall, for there is a "time and season for everything," when it comes the white oppressor must suffer silently.

---

[93] Frantz Fanon. *The Wretched of the Earth*. New York:1963, P.86

> Even if the knife is at the belly, let the white Christian not protest. Let him receive the assault recklessly, without precaution, without resistance, without rationalization, without extenuation, without a murmur.[94]

On the surface this appears a ridiculous notion, but the person making the "notion," is aware that "God has not forsaken the Cross." Only the oppressors have. Then he closes with the reason for his "notion."

> ... There is *no other* way that this enormous, desperate, growing accumulation of guilt, shame, estrangement, and terror can be absolved. There never has been – for any man, anywhere, at any time – any other way. In the work of God in our midst, reconciling black men and white men, there is no escape from the Cross.[95]

Will the oppressor go to the cross willingly, or will the tides of liberation drag him to the cross as he struggles to avoid it? That answer we do not have, but we can rest assured, there is no escaping the Cross. You see, the God of the oppressed is a just God. He is an "eye for an eye God. He is a "you reap what you sow," God. Therefore, there is no escape from the blood of the Cross-for anyone.

James Baldwin pronounced as confidently as a prophet of old, that destruction could be averted, only if those who have reached the level of understanding can convince the oppressors to end their game of oppression, or else.

---

[94] William Stringfellow. *Dissenter in a Great Society*. New York:1966, p.122
[95] Ibid., p.122

Everything now, we must assume, is in our hands; we have no right to assume otherwise. If we-and now I mean the relatively conscious whites and the relatively conscious blacks, who must, like lovers, insist on, or create, the consciousness of the others-do not falter in our duty now, we may be able, handful that we are, to end the racial nightmare, and achieve our country, and change the history of the world. If we do not now dare everything, the fulfillment of that prophecy, re-created from the Bible in song by a slave, is upon us: *God gave Noah the Rainbow sign, No more water, the fire next time.*[96]

When the divine fires have cleansed the guilt from the hearts and souls of the oppressors, and has seared the wounds of hate, fear and debasement from the psyche of our oppressed black people, we must rise like the phoenix, and seize control of the new Garden of Eden.

---

[96]James Baldwin. *The Fire Next Time*. New York:1963, Pp.121,122

Chapter 7

Black Queen
And The New Garden of Eden

After the New Garden has been appropriated and secured, one of the first things that must occur before the black queen can be elevated to her throne is the transformation of the black man. We must be transformed because of our past and present conditioning; we are too weak to lift her to the height required of her queenly glory. Our transformation process will begin during the struggle to liberate the Garden, but shall continue eternally, so we must keep what needs changing in the process of becoming that which God created us to be.

Transformation Of The Black Man

The Holy Bible of Christianity instructs us on how we may evidence the will of God in our lives. God's will for us, is for us to be what we are supposed to be. To strive to let the particular light that has been bestowed on us to shine and chase darkness out of the life of others. Currently, most of us are bankrupt in the light department. We don't have any light we can share with anyone. We are in need of light ourselves. We had the light at one time in our history, but we exchanged it for the darkness of the world. The light that was within became dimmer and dimmer as the power that energized it was depleted in the struggle with the outside forces of darkness. Too soon the light was extinguished and in rushed darkness. St Paul instructs us in the following Biblical scripture how to become that light again.

> And do not be conformed to this world, but be transformed by the renewing of your mind, that you may prove what the will of God is, that which is good and acceptable and perfect.[97]

We are admonished in the referenced text to stop imitating and being copies of the external forces of reality. We are directed to reject the images the world projects for us to imitate, or we run the risk of becoming like the world. When we become like the world, we suffer the pain from its "slings and arrows."

We are constantly agonizing because we are relentlessly attempting to become what we can't become. It is a dream that cannot become a reality, and is soon reduced to hopeless-ness in the face of opposition from the powerful forces of racism. In order for us to rid ourselves of our hopeless state it is necessary to eliminate the cause of it. Our hopeless state is caused by the tremendous amount of frustration accumulated from struggling with our backs against the wall, trying to be accepted by white racists as their brothers and equals, but after, finally realizing it is unobtainable, we come to know that the solution is in the total rejection of the dream. Then, we begin to understand that we must stop trying to be like someone else, spiritually,[98] or physically[99] and begin to be ourselves, and then, powers we never dreamed we had will be at our disposal.[100]

---

[97] Romans 12:2

[98] We must stop imitating and internalizing the values of others that are detrimental to us black people.

[99] Skin bleachers and hair straighteners in attempts to acquire the looks of others.

[100] The powers our ancient African ancestors had at their disposal when constructing the awesome pyramids and the mysterious sphinx that stares towards the east. The powers that made possible our ability to create the world's most ancient, and grandest civilizations.

After the total rejection of the external racist stimulus, we are to "be transformed by the renewing your Mind." We are to become changed by filling our minds with new thoughts. We need to fill our minds with thoughts and images of us that say we are the, 'original man,' and 'creators of Egyptian and all great ancient civilizations,' also 'the survivors of the trial by fire,' and 'creators of the sciences;' 'music' and ultimately the "saviors of the world.' For you see, a "man is as he thinketh." We have within the depths of our essential selves the Spirit of God that is awaiting its manifestation to the world through our particularity. We can never know our full potential selves until we manifest and reveal the Divine Being that resides within. However, this is rather difficult while we are oppressed by the image of something we can't become. We end up replacing the self that should be revealed to the world with an alien counterfeit self. This image must be rejected, and the divine image that is within must be given support for its natural growth and unfolding as it acquiesces to its divine purpose in life. Our mission quite simply is to become what God created us to become by allowing the Divine Spirit that dwells within to have its own way.

I have no particular theory about the exact form and content, or type of governing system we should utilize in our own self-determining political territory. However, I do believe that the proper ideological reference for us to use in problem solving will develop in the context of the coming revolution. I hope that new world I am struggling for will be grounded in sister and brotherhood. I believe one road to making that goal a reality, is paved with a viable value system that supports brother and sisterhood. One such system has already been laid at the heart of many of our people. It is called, *The Nguza Saba*.

Dr Maulana Karenga has provided us with a value system that promotes excellence and brotherhood.

Nguzo Saba (7 principles)

UMOJA- (Unity)-To strive for and maintain unity in the family, community, nation and race.

KUJICHAGULIA -(self-determination) -To define ourselves, create for ourselves and speak for ourselves, instead of being defined, named, created for, and spoken for by others.

UJIMA- (Collective Work & Responsibility)-To build and maintain our community together and to make our sisters and brothers problems our problems and to solve them together.

UJAMAA- (Co-operative Economics)-To build and maintain our own stores, shops, and other businesses and to profit from them together.

NIA- (Purpose)-To make as our collective vocation the building and developing of our community in order to restore our people to their traditional greatness.

KUUMBA- (Creativity)-To always do as much as we can, in the way we can in order to leave our community more beautiful and beneficial than when we inherited it.

IMANI- (Faith)-To believe with all our hearts in our people, our parents, our teachers, our leaders and the righteousness and victory of our struggle.[101]

Black Family In The New Garden

The natural state of man and woman is unity. They were created in unity, and both derived from a single entity. This entity is identified as Adam in the Judeo/ Christian context. The

---

[101] Maulana Karenga.. September 7:1965

physical separation into male and female is described in the Book of Genesis, in the Christian Holy Bible.

> 21 So the Lord caused a deep sleep to fall upon the man, and he slept; then He took one of his ribs, and closed up the flesh at that place.
> 22 And the LORD God fashioned into a woman the rib which He had taken from the man, and brought her to the man.
> 23 And the man said, "This is now bone of my bones, And flesh of my flesh; She shall be called Woman, Because she was taken out of Man."[102]

Since this separation, man and woman have always been drawn towards each other spiritually and physically. The driving force behind their relationship appears to be a primordial desire to merge and once again become as one. The Bible insists,

> For this cause a man shall leave his father and his mother, and shall cleave to his wife; and they shall become one flesh.[103]

The concept and model for the family and state should be based on the traditional family of Africa whose foundational centrality of marriage provides for unity and equality of male with the female in its broader sense, as informer John S Mbiti describes it in his ground-breaking and authoritative, *African Religions and Philosophy*.

---

[102] Gen 2:21-23
[103] Genesis 2:24

> We must note also that marriage and procreation in African communities are a unity: without procreation marriage is incomplete. This is a unity which attempts to recapture, at least in part, the lost gift of immortality of which we spoke in chapter nine. It is a religious obligation by means of which the individual contributes the seeds of life towards man's struggle against the loss of original immortality. Biologically both husband and wife are reproduced in their children, thus perpetuating the chain of humanity. In some societies it is believed that the living dead are reincarnated in part, so that aspects of their personalities or physical characteristics are 'reborn' in their descendants. A person who, therefore, has no descendants in effect quenches the fire of life, and becomes forever dead since his line of physical continuation is blocked if he does not get married and bear children. This is a sacred understanding and obligation which must neither be abused nor despised.[104]

This African philosophy reminds the black man and woman of their basic unity and their total need for and dependence on one another, if they are to travel the road of immortality. Without the black woman, the black man, and race would become extinct. That's how much we need each other. Very simply stated, if there is no black queen, there will be no black king.

---

[104] Joseph s Mbiti. *African Religions and Philosophy*. Great Britain:1989, p.133.

Democracy In The New Garden

By democracy, I certainly don't mean the kind of democracy practiced in the United States of America. It appears to be the perfect form of government in its written form and verbalizations; however, it has not been realized in practice. Maybe I shouldn't dismiss this kind of democracy, just because I have never experienced it. Maybe it just doesn't apply to me, which doesn't mean it can't work. Any system will work if the people will it to work. Do we want a democracy? Maybe some of us want a monarchy, or socialism, or communism, or some other yet to be defined ism. The name of the thing is important, but not as important as the thing itself. Is a rose by any other name, still a rose? Does it still smell the same? If it has a foundation based on sister, and brotherhood, let's give it a try.

Pan-Africanist scholar, Chancellor Williams provides a very practical definition of democracy that should provide, and evidence true brotherhood.

> Democracy then, at its best, is a system working out the humane idea of equality of rights, equal justice, and equality of opportunity. This last is equality of rights as a principle translated into an actual, practical system that insures individual freedom and the fullest opportunity to develop, serve and be rewarded according to one's talent, character and will. This kind of democracy, moving from a mere ideal and principle to a way of life will, in any one nation, become a vast extended family where the spirit of brotherhood and sisterhood is the determining factor in the

complex and often conflicting interests that develop in human relations.[105]

Education

Many of our scholarly leaders, notably Dr. Carter G Woodson,[106] have spoken, or written about the miss-education of the African American. It appears that something, or someone has drained our minds of the knowledge of our history and past accomplishments, and filled our skulls with a world-view* and ideology that destroys our self-esteem and humanness. If we are to really liberate ourselves, we must first liberate our minds. We must free our minds of all the oppressive, symbols (verbal and audio) that point us towards an ideology that embraces, and fosters self-hatred and ultimately, self-destruction of Africans everywhere.

When we (black males) begin school we are mentally ahead of the other children, but by the 4th grade,[107] we have descended to the bottom of the echelon. Something drastic occurs, that demotivates the black male child by the time he is ten years old. We need to focus on the problem and work to resolve it. There appears to be a conspiracy to destroy black boys. Someone or something wants to destroy their minds. This is accomplished in various ways, but mostly thru the various media utilizing symbols and the racist tool of preventing the possibility of mental growth, and is maintained by discrimination and segregation. Physical gymnastics are okay, but mental ones discouraged. The black man's mind must be kept in chains, because if it becomes liberated he will take over the world.

---

[105] Chancellor Williams. *Re-birth of African Civilization*. VA:1993, P.133
[106] Carter G Woodson. *Miss-Education of the Negro*.
* Eurocentrism.
[107] See: Jawara Kunjufu. *Conspiracy to Destroy Black Boys*.

Mae Gadpaille, the noted African American, Montessori Method educator, insists on the following.

> ...we have a mind that is superior, really a superior mind. That is why the whites fight us all the time. They don't want that mind to show forth its greatness.[108]

We cannot sit back and allow others to influence us to use our minds against ourselves. We must seize control of the education of our children and direct them and consequently, us into another direction.

Education should be mandated. Everybody should be required to attend school for a required minimum number of years, unless mental or physical limitations as determined by the citizenry prevents attendance. If incapacitation is the case, then alternative ways and methods should be put in place to insure an educated generation. This important aspect of our continuing struggle towards perfection requires the use of a revolutionary approach, which exploits the premise that each individual comes to the learning process with all the knowledge from their ancestors compressed in a vast memory bank that reaches back to the first human beings. Each one has within themselves the seed of what they are to be. A tiny acorn appears very different from a mighty oak tree, but it has the potential within to become an oak tree, if the outside dynamics allows for its growth and unfolding. With this concept we must prepare to unlock those vast reservoirs of eternal knowledge located within, rather than force indoctrination in alien ideology, and psychology on the mind from the outside environment. This kind of education will ultimately assist in unlocking the door that will liberate all of that suppressed knowledge that will

---

[108] P.42. Uraeus. Vol 2 Number 3. Third issue, 1982

allow for the rebuilding of a new civilization based on love, brother and sisterhood.

Black women will be queens again, but they will understand that black queens are so, because there are black kings. We black kings will understand that we wouldn't be black kings if it wasn't for black queens. Then we will be ready to usher in a new world, based on a new foundation of love, and unity.

Bibliography

Ani, Marimba, *Yurugu*. N.J:1994
Baldwin, James. *The Fire Next Time*. N.Y:1963. S.F:1965
Brinson, Rev John D. *Reparations! And God's Judgment*. 2002
Browne, Robert s., and Vernon, Robert. *Should the U.S. Be Partitioned*. N.Y:1968
Diop, Cheikh A. *African Origin of Civilization*. Westport:1974
Drake, St Clair. *Black Folk Here and There*. L.A:1987
Dubois, WEB. *Black Reconstruction*. N.Y:1935
Elkins, Stanley. *Slavery*. N.Y:1963
Fanon, Frantz. *The Wretched of the Earth*. N.Y:1968
Genovese, Eugene. *Roll Jordan Roll*. N.Y:1976
Goodrich, L. *Priestesses*. N.Y:1989
Grier, Cobb. *Black Rage*. 1968
Gutman, H.G. *The Black Family in Slavery and Freedom*. N.Y:1977
Hennessey, J.P. *A Study of the Atlantic Slave Trade*. N.Y:1967
Holy Bible. *NIV*. Grand Rapids:1997
Howell, Clark. *Life Nature Lib. Early Man*. N.Y:1965
Howell, D.W. *I was a Slave*. Wash:1996.
Jones, James. *Bad Blood*. N.Y:1981
Joyner, Charles. *Down By the Riverside*. Chicago:1985
Madhubuti, H. *Clash of the Races*. Chicago:1978
Liebow, *Talley's Corner*. Boston:1967
Madow, Leo. *Anger*. N.Y:1972
Mellon, James. *Bull Whip Days*. N.Y:1988
Memmi, Albert. *The Colonizer and The Colonized*. N.Y:1965

_____. *Dominated Man*. Boston:1968

Moore, Richard B. *The Name Negro: Its Origin and Evil Use*. Boston:1960
Means, Sterling. *Ethiopia and The Missing Link in African History*. Penn:1945
Myrdal, Gunnar. *An American Dilemma*. N.Y:1944
Nelson, Truman. *The Right to Revolution*. Boston:1968
Newton, John. *Thoughts Upon the African Slave Trade*. London:1788
Obadele, Imari Abubakari. *Foundations of The Black Nation*. S.F:1975
Pettigrew, T.F. *A Profile of The Negro American*. Princeton:1964
Stampp, Kenneth M. *The Peculat Institution*. N.Y:1956
Stringfellow, William. *Dissenter in a Great Society*. N.Y:1966
Williams, Michael s. *Genesis Revisited*. 2001

www.ingramcontent.com/pod-product-compliance
Lightning Source LLC
Chambersburg PA
CBHW050832160426
43192CB00010B/1996